"The stories in *Class Lessons* go beyond the [ ]
school experience and reveal heart-wrenching
trying to survive impossible and often horrifying situations, and the
dogged frustration and hope of a career educator trying her best to make
a difference. An indelible collection that sheds light on the limitations
of modern-day schooling, and the lives of vulnerable students who are
lost within it."

Hollay Ghadery, author of *FUSE*, *Rebellion Box*, and
Widow Fantasies

"An empathetic, caring and enthusiastic supporter of all those in her
care, Ms. Black shares stories of her interactions with young people,
many of whom are products of unhappy homes at all economic, social
and cultural levels. In my experience, these students are not the
exception; they represent a tiny segment of the youth affected by the
stressors in our homes and communities today. Even with the many
partner agencies attached to our public education sector, our schools are
not equipped to support successfully the youth living in dysfunctional
families. *Class Lessons* is a cry for help!"

Judy Bear, educator, academic services, Durham Catholic
District School Board

"I read. I wept. I turned the page and wondered where Gemma, Katie,
and their peers were now. 'Watching the thrust and parry of students,'
as Black does so well, is not the same as persuasively recreating that
thrust and parry but is the necessary first step, the moment of recognition
that only a wise teacher foresees. Black is a brilliant writer. She knows
the ropes of the school system from the inside—like blending history
and geography into a new genre. Her eye goes immediately to students
who lean out, who cross over, and who cannot let go of sorrow or escape
its wily traps. *Class Lessons: Stories of Vulnerable Youth* is a visionary
collection of stories. The vulnerable heroes are more attractive because
they are young folks in our midst facing a complicated and striated
world—by most accounts, the world we have both knowingly and
unknowingly made for them."

Marlene Kadar, senior scholar and professor emerita,
Department of Humanities and School of Gender, Sexuality, and
Women's Studies, York University, Toronto

"Within Lucy E. M. Black's fiction, the reader quickly becomes invested in her characters. *Class Lessons: Stories of Vulnerable Youth*, a collection of fictionalized accounts based on Ms. Black's career as an administrator in the public education system, takes on a poignant urgency that leaves the reader horrified, angry, and sickened by the life stories of students, and particularly young women. She worked with many support systems. Still, for some students, trying to cope with school and life, no manner of resources or care could protect them or direct them onto a trajectory to a happy ending. This haunting work is a witness and testimony to the author's love for the vulnerable students who came under her care."

Gail Kirkpatrick, author of *Sleepers and Ties*

CLASS
LESSONS

STORIES OF **VULNERABLE YOUTH**

Lucy E.M. Black

DEMETER

Class Lessons
Stories of Vulnerable Youth
Lucy E.M. Black

Demeter Press
PO Box 197
Coe Hill, Ontario
Canada
K0L 1P0
Tel: 289-383-0134
Email: info@demeterpress.org
Website: www.demeterpress.org

Demeter Press logo based on the sculpture "Demeter" by Maria-Luise Bodirsky
www.keramik-atelier.bodirsky.de

Printed and Bound in Canada

Cover design: Michelle Pirovich
Typesetting: Michelle Pirovich
Proof reading: Jena Woodhouse

Library and Archives Canada Cataloguing in Publication
Title: Class lessons: stories of vulnerable youth / by Lucy E.M. Black.
Names: Black, Lucy E. M., 1957- author
Description: Includes bibliographical references.
Identifiers: Canadiana 20240465202 | ISBN 9781772585063 (softcover)
Subjects: LCSH: Youth with social disabilities—Education. | LCSH: Students with social disabilities. | LCSH: Education—Social aspects.
Classification: LCC LC4065.B53 2024 | DDC 371.826/94—dc23

 The publisher gratefully acknowledges the support of the Government of Canada

The events, places, and conversations in this collection of stories are fictionalized for narrative purposes. Any resemblance to actual persons, living or dead, is entirely coincidental.

To educators and other professionals who give
unselfishly in the service of youth.

And to Madisson—wherever you are.

Foreword

These reflections describe the limitations of public education, teachers, and school administrators. But remember that our secondary schools are a cross-section of the community. Therein are thousands of dedicated educators, like Lucy Black, who take on all comers with the singular purpose of mentoring the development of each teenager into a productive and resourceful citizen. These reflections capture the failures that haunt long after Black's retirement. She continues to ponder how better outcomes could have been achieved. While these stories of failure are tragic, each reflects a sterling level of devotion and resourcefulness. Make no mistake, this is the same commitment made to every student, most of whom thrive and grow.

Many profiles reference other school and community resource personnel who may be called upon to offer guidance and assistance. The efforts of these folks are viewed as invaluable. Like any resource, the availability of such helpers is limited. Perhaps, Lucy Black's account may cause those in positions of influence to ponder the human and financial costs of maintaining those who fall through the cracks in the school system for a lifetime.

Dr. Joseph Allin, former assistant director of York Region District School Board and former chair of Durham District School Board

Preface

I was proud to be a career educator for twenty-nine years. I felt privileged to serve an organization that did so much good for many students. Unfortunately, school success is not experienced by all students, especially those for whom the struggles of daily existence overwhelm every other aspect of life. In my experience, female students are frequently among the most vulnerable yet the most resilient of such constituents.

These fictionalized stories bear witness to some of the trauma I have seen young people attempt to navigate, sometimes successfully and often with great difficulty. Although these stories arise from my encounters, they are not unique to any school or demographic. I believe that narratives such as these unfold in schools everywhere.

I do not share these narratives to be salacious or shocking. Rather, I intend to shine a spotlight on the vulnerability of youth, particularly young girls, living in poverty or heartbreaking circumstances beyond the scope of their control. It is vital to uphold the work taking place in schools and outside the classroom and embrace the support systems shared between the school and the community. We can make a lasting and positive difference in the lives of vulnerable young people through these joint commitments.

Contents

ORIGIN
STORIES

The Parking Garage

The steel door slammed behind me, and a sudden current of air licked the back of my legs. I stepped into the dank parking garage and hesitated before moving away from the entrance. The smell of stale urine and the stench from puddles of gas and oil hung in the air. I blinked while my eyes adjusted to the yellow lighting. There was a dripping sound coming from somewhere. I had been teaching crafts at the youth centre and had stayed late to help a couple of boys finish stamping their leather belts. Usually, the other staff members walked out with me, but on this night, I was alone, and my footfalls fell noisily. As I moved into the space, the broken lines of remaining cars suddenly revealed a figure wearing a ball cap darting behind a pillar. I felt goosebumps rise, and my skin prickled uncomfortably.

Key extended, I ran to my car and thrust it into the lock. The lock didn't turn. In my earlier hurry, I must have left it unlocked. Trembling, I ripped the heavy door open and stumbled inside, pulling it shut quickly, and locking myself in. I had forgotten to check the backseat. I tilted the mirror to check behind me. I didn't see anyone inside the car, but I glimpsed a crouched figure ducking only a row away. My hand began to shake, and I concentrated on putting the key in the ignition. I missed the key slot. Once. Twice. The third try connected.

Though not religious, I began to pray out loud, attempting to invoke a higher power. *Hail Mary, full of grace, the Lord is with you.* But only a few of the words came to me. I shifted the car into gear. The transmission clunked heavily. *Angel of God, my guardian dear. God's love for me has sent you here.* I navigated the garage as carefully and as quickly as I could. My foot uneven on the gas pedal, I headed towards the exit. *Our Father, who art in heaven.* My old university clunker had no power steering, and

I had to crank the wheel hard, hand over hand, while I made the final turn towards the ramp. My arms and legs were quivering. I was perspiring.

As I approached the bottom of the steep incline, the window in the driver's door dropped down into the door panel. Although this was a frequent occurrence, the suddenness of the vibration sickened me. I felt betrayed by my car. I began to coach myself, speaking aloud in the quiet. *You can do this. You know how to drive. It's not far now.* I floored the gas pedal. At street level, I heard the satisfying sound of the garage door as it rumbled closed behind me.

Still shaking, I navigated the streets homewards. I sat for a moment in the driveway, waiting for the tingling of adrenaline to dissipate. The back garden and an oversized cedar hedge separated our house from the garage. I walked to the house along the road, avoiding the shadows, and then ran the last few steps to the back entrance. Once inside, I locked and bolted the door and turned on all of the lights. I was clammy and still stinging with traces of fear.

In the morning, I lay in bed, remembering my panic. The pink and orange colours of my room made the parking garage seem far away. Someone had been hiding there, but I had no reason to believe he meant me harm. Despite having sensed danger, my fears were no doubt unfounded. I got out of bed to shower and dress before joining my parents at the breakfast table. I greeted them brightly. They had finished eating but were still seated at their places, listening to the morning news.

My father hadn't shaved. He was wagging his head in displeasure. His thickly accented voice bellowed at me. *You not going to that shelter again*, he decreed. *Enough.* He emphasized his point by raising his hand in a karate chop, striking the air definitively.

Why not? I bristled, as always, at his edicts.

Tell her! he said, commanding my mother.

Something happened last night. It was on the news. A girl was attacked in the parking garage, there, in that place where you go.

My stomach did a bellyflop. *My God. When? What time?*

Between 9:30 and 10:00 they said. She was badly hurt. You won't go anymore. It's not safe.

I was fine. I protested automatically but my voice was thin.

Fine. Schmine. Who knows who can be next? You think you know? He stood, angrily snatched his metal lunch pail and stomped down the hall. My mother padded after him. She returned quickly and sat at the table with me. I flushed under her gentling.

I think I saw him.

Mein Gott! Tell me.

When I was getting in my car to leave, I felt something. Voicing the story made me tremble anew. I squeezed my eyes shut, trying to control my tears.

Vooraf gevoeld (premonition), she gripped the side of the table. She paled; her fine freckles suddenly became defined and dark.

I saw a man hiding behind a pillar and running behind the cars, down low. He was wearing dark clothes and a baseball cap. That's all. A couple of glimpses. But something didn't feel right. And then my car window dropped down again, and I was really frightened.

And you're just telling me now? Why not wake us when you come in?

I thought I was being stupid.

Your father is right. No more volunteering.

But...

You heard your father. You call, and you tell them.

I felt like a coward, but I was also relieved.

Weeks later, and only a mile from the centre, a teenage girl was attacked after taking the bus. The driver described him as a white male, wearing dark blue clothing, with a baseball cap pulled down low. He saw him get up and suddenly exit the bus after the girl. The driver thought nothing of it until the police spoke to him during his next shift. The girl had been followed for only half a block before being dragged into bushes where she was beaten unconscious and raped. The news was full of the story. There was a predator in our neighbourhood. Two incidents only weeks apart. It would be years before any of us heard anything else about those attacks.

My father now insisted on driving me in the evenings when I went out. My boyfriend escorted me home from our dates in an act of unusual gallantry. I cringed at having to curtail my independence, explain myself, and make arrangements for male accompaniment. I bought a rape whistle and attached it to my keyring. I listened to all of the conflicting advice: *be compliant and don't provoke violence, scream bloody murder and fight, take self-defence lessons, don't take risks, be on guard.* I stopped running in the evening. *He could pull you in the bushes. He's done it before.* I stopped going for country drives alone with my camera. *Your car could break down. Anything could happen.* The fear rippled.

Several years later, the news reported that two missing schoolgirls had been abducted, tortured, and murdered. The police speculated that the accused had begun his trajectory long before, with unchecked offences that had continued to escalate. Everyday brought disturbing updates. The two unsolved attacks in our neighbourhood were among many being looked at by the police as a part of his escalation. I broke out in chills when I realized how close I had likely been to the girls' killer. Looking back, I now realize that all of the protective measures put in place to protect girls and women were also the things that constrained us and impinged upon our freedoms.

The Wrapper

In a previous career, I was the training manager for a large retail conglomerate that owned several chains of specialty stores. We only sold luxury goods. The stores were filled with sparkle and shine, wishes and dreams. Anything could be designed and purchased for a price. Sales associates kept careful records of client birthdays and anniversaries to prompt husbands with preselected tokens of love for wives, daughters, and lovers. The carpets were Persian, and the woodwork was burnished.

The elevator, complete with its chandelier and richly upholstered chairs, was discreetly tucked away in the corner of the sales floor and was used to whisk purchases downstairs for wrapping. Several stories below store level was a catacomb of sorts: vaults where the uncut gems were stored, a warehouse for the silver, and a design studio for the jewellers who crafted the custom pieces, offices, and other unique facilities required for our expert services. Only those with designated security levels, using retina scans and fingerprints, could access these areas. Above these chambers was another level, and it was here that the wrappers worked.

A small crew of individuals laboured in the depths, standing ready to wrap champagne flutes, silver trays, diamond tiaras, jewelry, exotic leather bags, small sculptures, and figurines. Empty linen-covered boxes of all sizes were piled on skids waiting to be filled. Bleached tissue, Styrofoam peanuts, and adhesive seals were amassed at the huge wrapping stations—ten-foot square tables centred under bright lighting. It was here that discrete price tags were removed. Each item was wiped clean of fingerprints or smudges, polished and then carefully blanketed in tissue. When a box was packed, pristine tissue was neatly folded and sealed. No tape was ever used.

The store had a distinct wrapping paper, distinctly patterned with the company's embossed logo. The gift box was then crisply covered in the paper, seams sharply creased, and tied up tightly with a cord. The cord was knotted and held in place with yet another seal. To look at a parcel finished in this way was to recognize the effort and expense that had gone into both its purchase and packaging.

A waiting sales associate, elegantly attired, would then take the package upstairs to their customer, delicately exchanging a sales receipt for a cheque or bank card to complete the transaction. There was a hushed, almost reverent quiet to such interactions, instilling a sense of old-world glamour and opulence. By contrast, workers four stories below were outfitted in canvas coveralls for the men and long canvas coats for the women. This silent, invisible staff polished the trays, cleaned the rings, repaired the watches, buffed the furniture, and wrapped the parcels.

Meeka was the head wrapper. A woman in her thirties, her chewed fingernails and pock-mocked face suggested a life that had been hard. Her blonde hair was always tightly tied in a ponytail, but the dark roots and underside revealed a badly done home-dye job. She wore thick pancake makeup, but the unevenness of her complexion was evident, marring what might otherwise have been a pleasant face, and she used too much foundation for daywear. Her eyeshadow and pencilled brows were done with a heavy hand. It sounds petty, but her lack of judgment about such things, not to mention wearing white pumps even in winter, set her apart. She was not invited to join the others for tea breaks or lunch. Even those condemned to labour in the labyrinth of cellars knew that Meeka was different. Snide comments about her weekend activities were often made and not always outside of her hearing.

But I liked her. Hers was always the company I sought when I went down below. She was open with me, generous with her updates, and candid about the day's events, such as the backlog of orders and the challenges of the workload. Although I taught new employees how to wrap parcels, Meeka was my first teacher. We spent a week together when I began, refining my knotting techniques and practising the wrapping of enormous crystal carvings, delicate bud vases, and diamond bracelets. She would not let a parcel leave the wrapping area unless each crease was sharp, each knot tight, and each seal perfectly positioned. Her meticulous scrutiny had long since made me a fan.

Meeka, like the others in their drab canvas casings, was not permitted on the showroom floor. She envied my ability to ride the elevator and navigate between the two worlds. It was not the status, responsibility, or even the salary of my position she coveted but rather the simple freedom to walk through the heavy brass doors and luxuriate in the surroundings of beautiful objects. She told me this one long night while we were wrapping dozens of watches for a corporate client. Her shy admission slipped out.

You are so lucky, she sighed as I, burdened by parcels, was about to go upstairs.

What do you mean?

You get to go upstairs. To take the elevator.

I was in a hurry and took my bundle without responding but I thought about what she had said. Although I and all of the management and the floor staff routinely used the front doors, those who worked below grade were expected to travel a long maze of dimly lit concrete tunnels from the loading dock, past the garbage bins, to arrive at work. The inequity of such treatment was shocking. I had questioned it when I first arrived and was told: *We can't have just any slag just walking through our doors. We are not that kind of establishment. Appearance is everything in our business. There would be huge security issues.*

To be blunt, Cathy, the HR manager, was a pretentious snob. Educated at a private girls' college, she emitted an air of haughty arrogance. She dressed in sombre plaid skirts and oversized blazers, and one had the sense that she had never deviated far from her school uniforms. Her thin hair was cut in a short bowl with a ridge of bangs that touched the top of her round glasses. Having worked for the organization for so long, she had absorbed its ethos so completely that she acted as though the world below stairs was not worth mentioning. I often found her unhelpful and tried, as best I could, to stay out of her way. *Security issues* was her fallback position for anything she did not want to support. Not inviting the wrappers and cleaners to our corporate Christmas party, for instance, was, in Cathy's words, for *security issues.* It made no sense but indicated the discussion was closed.

When I next saw Meeka, I sidled up beside her while she was working and asked her to have lunch with me. She agreed but said that she would have to meet me outside, as we could not be seen leaving the store together. I understood this, and we met at a small bistro near the store.

Meeka, tell me how you came to be a wrapper.

I was sixteen, just a kid, and my old man told me there was a job cleaning shit at the store. I don't know how he heard about it. I started as a cleaner, working steady nights. But then a junior wrapping position came up, and I applied for it. I don't know why, but I got the job. And after a few years, the head wrapper job came up. Marjory had angina and decided to retire, and she recommended me. She must have pushed for me. I've worked for the company for fifteen years. It's a good job.

If you could do anything else with your life, what would it be?

I'd work on the showroom floor. Maybe at the watch counter or in men's goods. Nothing too grand. I'd like to ride up and down in the elevator and wear nice clothes and not have to stay in the basement.

Have you ever applied for a sales job?

Yeah. Once. There was an ad in the paper for seasonal help. I thought I'd try.

What happened?

Miss Wilks asked a lot of questions I couldn't answer. And then she told me I'd have to quit my wrapping job. And there was no guarantee I'd ever get that job back. And so, I was stuck. She said it was better to keep a sure thing.

I'm surprised.

Really? Why?

I thought HR would want to encourage employees to try new things and broaden their horizons. I'm just surprised.

I have a good job. I couldn't risk losing it. My old man wouldn't be happy.

Are you married then?

No. Bill don't believe in that. He has a mean temper, but he looks after me.

When we got back to the store, I called Cathy from my office. I was annoyed.

I had lunch with Meeka today, and she told me that she tried to be in sales.

Yes.

And you actively discouraged her?

Yes. Of course. We'd never hire her sort for the showroom.

What do you mean by that? Her sort?

Really? Get off your sanctimonious horse. You can clearly see that she's not the right fit.

I don't see actually. Why couldn't she try working in watch repair or returns?

That will never happen.

I could help her.

And who will wrap? Who will do her job? And what will you tell the president the first time she flips a bird at a customer, chews gum on the showroom floor, or cusses out a customer? I won't risk it.

You're in HR, and you won't even give her a chance?

You don't know what you're dealing with. Do you know what she does when her boyfriend needs some extra cash? He sends her out on the street!

How do you know that?

Because she's been seen. By the men in shipping and in the warehouse. There have been many reports over the years. Now, if you don't mind, I have real work to do.

I admit I was a little dumbfounded. Cathy was all kinds of a bitch, but I didn't think she was a lying bitch. I had no reason not to believe her. It actually explained the innuendos and comments I had heard whispered in nasty undertones. To my shame, I admit that I didn't seek out Meeka's company after that. I didn't avoid her particularly, but I didn't want to give her false hope either.

We were approaching the Mother's Day sales period. This was, by far, the peak selling season for the store, bigger than Christmas and Valentine's Day put together. As was corporate policy, this was the time of year when everyone in management was expected to help out on the showroom floor. I loved the change of pace and the opportunity to see the experienced sales associates hard at work. I had my own commission number but was careful not to steal sales away from the regular sales staff. I would ring up a respectable tally and then rush around trying to assist the others by taking their packages downstairs for wrapping.

One night, just before Mother's Day, I arrived downstairs to a scene of chaos. Meeka had not arrived at work, and the junior wrappers were completely disorganized without her. Their stations had not been replenished with tissue and other necessities, and they were shouting at one another, assigning blame.

Where's Meeka? I asked but no one knew. I assessed the situation and quickly assigned one of the junior wrappers the task of stocking the stations. Order was soon restored, but the staff phone was ringing incessantly. In great frustration, I picked it up.

Who is this? I barked, rather impolitely.

It's me, Meeka. I can't come in tonight.

Why on earth not? What's wrong? It's chaos here. You should have called in earlier.

He threw out all my clothes... I don't have anything to wear... I'm hurt... The voice was tiny, weak, and choked sounding.

Where are you? What happened? Who hurt you?

I have to go now...

She hung up the phone. *Fuck.*

I called Cathy at home and told her about the call. *What can we do? Can we call the police? Do you have her address?*

Don't bother yourself. She does this all the time. It's a ploy. She's overslept and doesn't want to get in trouble. There's nothing wrong with her. She'll be back at work tomorrow.

I felt uneasy just leaving things, but the rush of the store soon distracted me. I went to the store the next day, hoping to see Meeka. She didn't come in and didn't call. None of the other wrappers knew where she lived. I called Cathy again. *She's not here. We should call the police.*

They won't do anything. I told you she was a hooker. She's well known to them.

So, we're not going to do anything at all?

We're going to do our jobs.

Where does she live? I want to see her.

Somewhere in Moss Park. She never gave us a complete address. She's sneaky that way. You'll never find her.

After work, I took the Queen streetcar east. Looking back now, I don't know what I hoped to accomplish. As we drove past a towering apartment complex, I peered out the window, willing myself to see her. I didn't care if she was standing on a corner in her ridiculous white pumps hooking or hurrying somewhere with a bag of groceries. I just wanted to know that she was alright. It was naive, I admit. The streetcar moved on, and weary passengers continued to climb off and on at each stop. I finally rang the bell myself, knowing that it was time for me to go home. Meeka didn't return to the store, and I continued to miss her. Despite the privilege and wealth we were surrounded by, I hated that we did not have the humanity to care for those who existed outside our fragile boundaries.

We promoted one of the junior wrappers to head wrapper. She was a young girl, anxious to please, eager to impress, and nicely groomed. I knew that she would do well. After a year or two, she would likely be moved to the watch counter or men's goods.

Lena

I worked as a corporate trainer for several years before becoming a high school teacher. I loved the glamour of corporate training and the variety of jobs. One day I might be working with experienced salespeople on enhancements to their customer service, and the next I might be teaching part-time workers how to change the tapes in our clunky cash registers or grooming prospective store managers. The range of duties challenged me.

Head office was located out of province, and I was summoned to an elite resort for the annual retreat. Between cocktails, elaborate dinner parties and winter sports, we were encouraged to identify our top salespeople in each unit. These individuals were to participate in a new week-long course preparing them to become store managers.

I quietly questioned whether the types of people and personalities who were successful as commissioned salespeople would necessarily have the skill set or the desire to be store managers. The training was a prepackaged course purchased from an outside organization. We were given time to briefly review the modules, but the direction had been set and was not up for discussion. My reservation about the strategy notwithstanding, I was told to draw up a list of prospective candidates and establish a training schedule.

Back in my training room, I reviewed the sales figures from each store and selected the top candidates for the new training opportunity. Candidates reacted to the prestigious invitation in two ways. Most were flattered and excited, but some were concerned about their lost commissions during the training time. Only one individual turned me down flat. Her name was Lena, and not only was she the top salesperson for her store, she was the top salesperson for one of the chains she represented. I drove to meet her for a coffee and to discuss her refusal. I was certain that with gentle persuasion, she would agree to the training.

When I arrived, I saw Lena on the salesfloor. She was, as usual, behind the jewellery counter and had draped herself in several long strands of pearls. This was a practice encouraged by management as a way of showcasing beautiful pieces. Tight controls were in place, and only certain salespeople were allowed the privilege. Against the black of her well-cut dress, the lustre of the pearls appeared to exceptional advantage. Lena's dark hair was arranged on her head and held in place with a diamante comb. She was naturally slender and looked the epitome of grace and elegance.

I waited until there were no customers in sight before approaching her.

Good morning, Lena.

She looked up at me and grimaced.

I know why you're here.

Good. Then you'll have a cup of coffee with me.

I forced myself to emit a cheerful, perky vibe.

I really don't have time. I have a very busy morning.

I looked around the store pointedly. There were no potential customers in the area. Several salespeople were dusting counters and polishing the merchandise to keep themselves busy.

It's a momentary lull. I've been rushed off my feet until now.

Lena, really?!

All right. Just a minute.

She took off the pearl necklaces and returned them to a locked drawer. She signed the leather book to indicate that the stock had been returned. I leaned over the counter, signed as a witness, and wrote the time beside my name. This was only a precaution, of course. Each counter was equipped with a security camera, and the log book was only used as a quick reference point.

We took the elevator to the mezzanine and walked to a nearby coffee stand. The shopping mall was calm for the moment. Senior citizens in power-walking groups and young mothers pushing strollers seemed to comprise most of the crowd. We sat at a quiet table in the corner of the food court.

Lena, why are you so reluctant to take this course? Is it the loss of commissions? We can pay you a daily rate plus a per diem flat amount to help compensate for the loss. It might not be exactly what you would earn, but it's a lot of money and a really great career move.

I can't afford the financial hit.

I could arrange for you to take on some extra shifts to compensate?

No. I don't want to do that.

Lena, you're our top salesperson for the chain. It will look as though you've been passed over if you don't take the course. You know most of our managers are men. They'll say you couldn't cut it or that we didn't believe you could do it. You'll be discredited. We have exactly one female store manager right now. Out of how many? It's nuts. You have to do this and show those buggers what you're made of.

I saw her hesitate.

Let me think about it.

It starts next week. I need an answer today. We have to rework the schedule at the store to cover your shifts.

I'm not sure. Really. I don't want to do this.

What am I supposed to tell Danny, your store manager? He already thinks he's such hot shit. Am I supposed to tell him that you don't think you can run a store? That he's better than you? He'd love that.

It was manipulative as hell to talk about Danny in this way, but I knew that Lena had little respect for him. He was a pompous ass and often denigrated the women who worked for him.

No!

She looked defiant.

I'll do it. We both know that Danny's a patronizing prick. I won't give him the satisfaction.

Good! That's what I wanted to hear. You won't be sorry.

I wish that I hadn't pushed so hard and hadn't pressured her. I didn't realize that what happened next would change our lives.

The course began the following Monday in my training room. I emailed everyone a prework package, and we spent the first part of the morning reviewing goals and objectives. There were two dozen people in the course, and most of them knew each other, so there was a comfortable feeling in the room. After the break, I asked them to pull out their prework booklets so we could review some of their answers.

I read out the first question, which was a case work scenario: It was a "you are the store manager and this happens and that happens and what do you do in response" type of question. It was intended to reveal core priorities and values. We went around the room, and each of the participants read me their response. The group clapped enthusiastically after each response, I highlighted a key point or two, and we continued around the room. When it was Lena's turn, she blushed.

I forgot my glasses, and I can't read or write without them.

We skipped over her and moved on to the next participant.

After lunch, we did some role-playing, and everyone participated. Then I gave them their instructions for the rest of the afternoon. They were to each visit a retail store, purchase an item, and then return it without the bill, complaining about the quality. It didn't matter what store they went to, what they bought, or how much money they spent. They were to record their experiences, and we would review them the next morning.

On day two, we had a wonderful morning. We debriefed their shopping and return experiences and had a couple of great laughs together. Before we broke for lunch, I asked them to set out their workbooks, as we would spend the afternoon working on some written exercises. Lena stopped me on her way out.

I wasn't able to find my glasses. I can't read or write anything. Should I just go back to the store this afternoon?

Her words sounded casual enough, but I noted she was anxious, breathing rapidly and standing stiffly.

You can't really afford to miss any of the modules, Lena. If you do, I can't give you the completion certificate. Why not go to the drugstore and try to find a cheap pair of readers?

Uh, sure. Sure. I can try that. Good idea.

I smiled at her. Crisis averted, I thought.

When we began work in the afternoon, the others in the group began their task immediately. Heads bowed over their workbooks, they were focussed and on task while they wrote. I circulated the large room, casually checking in on everyone. When I got to Lena, I saw that she was struggling with her reading glasses. Bright red half-readers were perched on her nose, and she was sliding them closer and further along the bridge of her nose, attempting to focus.

I've bought the wrong ones, she said, looking at me with despair. *I can't see a damn thing.*

Leaning close, I whispered the instructions to her.

This is a case study. You are supposed to imagine that you are the store manager during an electrical power-out. What are your priorities? What are some of the protocols you must follow? What do you do with all the customers in the store? Try to jot down some points.

I moved on, satisfied with myself. When I walked away, she was uncapping a Montblanc fountain pen.

The writing activity took most of the afternoon. There were a number of follow-up questions for the case study, and many details that needed to be incorporated in the answer. I collected the workbooks when everyone left and said that I would review them in the evening. Lena was among the last to leave.

Sorry, she said handing me her book. *I couldn't see a thing.*

While she stood there, I flipped open her book and saw that she had spent the afternoon doodling on one of the pages. She had written down nothing in response to the case.

Sit down. I gestured back towards the table and chairs. I shut the door.

You didn't really forget your glasses, did you, Lena?

She shook her head slowly.

Can you read at all?

She shook her head again.

How do you manage at the store? I don't understand.

Slowly, she raised her face to look at me. She was frightened, and her eyelashes were wet with tears.

I take work home to my brother. Then I come back to the store. He reads to me and writes down what I say.

Is it just English? Can you read Italian?

Nothing.

She sobbed and looked down at the floor. Her shoulders were dejected. She looked ashamed. I felt responsible.

How did you get through school? You have to be a high school graduate to work in our stores. They called me a retard at school. I just stopped going. My brother filled out the application. We lied.

Oh, Lena. I'm so sorry you had that experience. You know, it's never too late. I bet I could find someone who could teach you. Would you be willing to try if I found someone?

Yes! I'm so tired of faking it... of pretending. And what will I do when Mario goes to college? No one else at home can read or write English.

Leave it with me, Lena. I'll need to make some calls. But I promise you, we'll find a solution.' Thank you for trusting me with your secret.

Will you have to tell?

Maybe one or two people at head office but not the store. Not Danny. I'll keep the secret as quiet as I can. I promise.

She hugged me tightly on her way out. This incredibly lovely and elegant woman had just told me her deepest secret, one that had shamed her for years, and she clung to me as if I had just saved her life. I was deeply moved.

Later that week, I called the local university and discovered that there was a private lab for adults with learning difficulties. One-on-one instruction was available in a three-month session with high success rates for dealing with adult literacy issues. It sounded perfect. The registration fee was steep, but with some finagling, I could cover the cost from my training budget. The outstanding issue was a human resources and payroll one. I would need permission to release her from the store for three months while still paying her a flat wage, without commissions.

Years before, I learned that managers don't want to hear about problems unless they are also brought a solution. I printed off pages of documentation about the program, including statistics about the success rates. I approached Cathy, the head of HR with my request. I was excited and expecting a pat on the back for having identified a problem and resolving it with such an effortless solution. Instead, I was astounded by her response.

Why would we do this? She's managed so far, and there's no reason why she shouldn't continue.

Cathy looked at me incredulously as if I had just suggested the most ludicrous thing in the world.

I stared at her, finally stammering out a shocked reply.

Her brother is going to college soon. He won't be able to help her for much longer.

She'll find someone else.

It's an investment in our employee. She's our top salesperson in the chain. Don't you want her to be a store manager?

Not really. What I want is her on the floor selling. We can't afford to take her off sales for three months. The numbers will take a downturn, and nobody wants that, do they?

Her tone was condescending and dismissive. I was completely taken aback by her unwillingness to consider it. I looked around her office, searching for something I could use in my argument. A display case of Moorcroft Pottery graced the corner behind her desk. I briefly wondered if it was from her collection, or if it came with the office. But there was nothing else. The walls were blank, and her desk was unadorned, with no pictures of loved ones, no clutter—just an expensive corner office with this owl-eyed woman dismissing me.

I don't understand. Why did I bother putting her through the new training modules?

It's like this. We had to be seen to be offering career opportunities. We've done that. But what we need most are healthy sales figures. That's what Lena provides. End of discussion.

You can't just say "no." It's cruel. She can't read, Cathy. How can you live with that?

Easily. It's not my problem!

She ran her fingertips along the edge of her desk blotter as if checking for dust. She examined them afterwards and rubbed her hands together, ridding them of invisible particles.

But it's mine. I'm in charge of training.

But you're not a kindergarten teacher. We don't pay you to teach the alphabet.

I'll go over your head.

Fine. Do it. The answer will be the same.

So it was. Despite my best efforts, I was turned down at the highest level, and I made an enemy in the process. Cathy did not forgive me for going over her head. Every little opportunity to undermine me in meetings or to criticize me to upper management was a fresh opportunity for her to exercise her spitefulness.

Lena was devastated when I broke the news to her. I had held out the magical promise of literacy and then had taken it away. She understood, of course. She was a professional and a good corporate employee. She had worked for the chain for twelve years and wasn't surprised. But I felt like dirt. It sucked the joy out of my job, and I lost all respect for senior management. My self-confidence took a shit-kicking. This was not the first time I had clashed with Cathy over important staff issues, but it was the last.

I knew that I would never feel good about the decision that was made or the people who made it. After a couple of all-nighters talking it through with my partner, I submitted my resignation. The company president was shocked. Mr. Bailey was an out-of-date, old boy from good schools. He lived in Rosedale and thought that women should never wear trousers. Despite his privileged and often archaic perspective on things, I had managed to earn a certain modicum of his respect. He couldn't understand why I was committing career suicide.

If you don't like training, we could use you in Yorkdale or Bloor. I know you're good on the floor, a pity to waste your abilities.

I knew that in his way, he meant the offer to be kind. And I knew that I would miss the glamour and security of my job, the prestige of my position, and the other employees who had become friends. I didn't have a next move in mind, and I was worried about personal finances, but I couldn't continue working in a place where I felt compromised and where something as important as employee literacy was devalued. I thanked him for the opportunity and left his office, aware that I was fortunate enough to have a choice.

Career Change

Carol was a former table dancer, who after a particularly bad encounter with her pimp-boyfriend-landlord had joined a government-subsidized employability skills program. She was well turned out: cream-coloured sandals, a ruffled, flowery dress, panty-hose, hair pulled back with a banana clip, and lightly-done makeup. The only off-note was her fingernails—shockingly long and tapered into bright red daggers. I was thrilled to see her looking so pulled together, except for those nails. It was a convincing transformation.

Her indignation was palpable. It was her first "on the books" job and paycheque. Carol was sitting across from me looking severely annoyed.

Did you know those pricks were going to take money from my pay?! What the fuck? I could make more on a good Saturday night than I made working two weeks answering the damn phones and doing all their other shit. How the fuck am I supposed to make rent?

Having left corporate training, I was now working with the federal government and a school board to develop a short program introducing unemployed adults to basic computer and work-related skills. I taught them how to use a computer, how to dress for success (with the help of clothing vouchers from a charity shop), and how to write a resume. I was particularly proud of the phrase "self-employed in the entertainment industry; experienced multi-tasker." I helped these women prepare for job interviews and placed them in work assignments where they received a modest income from their government-subsidized employers. Most were offered permanent contracts at the end of their placements. Despite their willingness to try a new direction, some, like Carol, found the meagre earnings insulting and difficult to live on. Unfortunately, almost 50 per cent of them dropped out of the program after the first month.

At that time in the nineties, appearances were much more regulated, and clothes really did make a difference. Miuccia Prada once said, *What you wear is how you present yourself to the world. Fashion is instant language.* Carol's earlier outfits included a sheer blouse and a leather miniskirt with fuck-me shoes; a bright bikini top with spandex pants and spikey heels; and a silver dress scooped low in the front and back, with a hemline that just barely covered the essentials. She had a great smile, a vivacious personality, and a distinctive style. At first, convincing her to use the charity shop vouchers to outfit her for the job assignment was a bit of a struggle, but she had relented and now, for the most part, blended into her new environment, with her new "boring" clothes.

I was in the midst of my career change. After clashing with the boss in my previous life, I abruptly quit my job and blew my career as a corporate trainer.

You have a teaching degree, why not use it to teach? said my partner.

But teaching school had never actually been on my radar. Earning a teaching degree had been about furthering my promotability as a trainer. Working with teenagers instead of senior executives and sales staff seemed to me to be a big leap, yet I had loved practice teaching.

I prepared a batch of application packages stressing my training expertise and volunteerism and was promptly scheduled for three interviews. The three interviews turned into two competing job offers. While I interviewed for one job in a pretty lakeside town, my partner viewed real estate ads in the window of a local office. Afterwards, we walked around the lake and park and said to each other, *we could live here, put down roots and have a family.* A new kind of life suddenly seemed possible. No more commutes to the city and the possibility of a quieter, more idyllic way of life. A slower pace. Even though it meant accepting a substantial cut in salary, it was an easy decision.

My first few months as a classroom teacher involved a steep learning curve. I tried, as much as possible, to emulate the business world in my interactions with my students. I kept office hours and expected them to make appointments for extra help. I taught them how to shake hands, write contracts, and negotiate due dates, marks, and rewards. In turn, many of them began to trust me with their secrets and burdens. A girl raped at a field party told me about it before she told her mother. A boy who had broken into an abandoned house to steal small items confessed to me before agreeing to turn himself in. A pregnant teen being forced by her religious parents to marry a boy she didn't love wept in my arms. A boy who drunkenly crashed his father's truck and blamed it on a deer confided the truth to me. All of these stories were openly shared with me in ways that I had not asked for. I suddenly found an entire dimension to my role as a teacher that I had not expected.

In between the lesson preparations and the endless marking, I fell in love with these young people and the job. I realized that I had found my thing in life. I could share my skills and might be able to do some good. After some of the unsavoury aspects of the corporate world, public service seemed appealing.

I taught high school for several years before I was recruited for the special assignment of working with adults. Years before, someone in the business world told me that one should never turn down a career-building opportunity. With some reluctance, I left the high school where I had been happy and took on the challenge of creating something new that would benefit those out of work—people who needed to learn new skills to change their lives.

And the stories and confidences kept coming. There was Lynn whose boyfriend had deliberately stabbed a box of condoms with a safety pin, ensuring that despite her efforts at protection, she would share his STD. Rita, who had a gambling addiction and was afraid to go home, having lost the rent money. And Paul, who along with a group of his friends had been laid off from a local stamping plant because they didn't have their high school diplomas. That group was willing to do anything we asked of them, eager to earn prior learning credits and their diplomas as quickly as possible.

The work was challenging and exposed me to a gritty aspect of life that from my reasonably sheltered background, I had never seen: drug addiction, alcoholism, mental health concerns, poverty, child abuse, and other difficult realities. It was also emotionally exhausting. Entering into the lives of so many people and trying to support them in practical ways stretched me thin. When I was asked to become an administrator, it seemed like a natural progression.

My first few weeks as a vice-principal were awful. I stood outside classroom doors and listened to those still teaching, thinking how much I wanted to be inside the room rather than outside. A huge part of being a high school vice-principal involves school discipline, and it was my job to assign detentions for misbehaviour, reprimand students who skipped class, and support teachers with classroom management problems. During those first early days, I was sworn at, threatened, and spat upon. As a job, it sucked, and I seriously contemplated quitting.

It didn't help that I was perpetually hungry. I needed to be at school at 7:00 a.m. to organize the supply teachers, so I packed a big lunch and snacks to get through the ten-hour day. But day after day, it disappeared. I kept an insulated lunch bag on a corner of my desk, and invariably when I returned to the office for something, I discovered that the bag was open, and the food was missing.

I started packing extra sandwiches and fruit, but they too disappeared. When speaking to a young boy in my office one day, I realized that he was not listening to me but was looking longingly at my lunch bag. I reached in and offered him a sandwich and apple, which he quickly snatched and secreted under his shirt. The penny dropped, and I realized students had been sneaking into my office and stealing my lunch. How could we expect students to concentrate on schooling when they were hungry was a question that needed to be addressed.

The woman I worked for gave me a challenge. She told me to spend ten minutes a day doing something I wanted to do, something I was passionate about, and something that would make a difference.

She said to me: *No matter how busy you get, make sure you always steal those ten minutes a day for you doing something you love.*

I used those ten minutes a day to form a community partnership that facilitated a free breakfast program for the school. When we saw kids sneaking in for food two and three times a morning, we also initiated a lunch program. And then came a clothing exchange and a wellness centre. Staff volunteered to help and supported all of the new initiatives. Encouraged by the turnaround in student behaviour and health and wellbeing, I saw how my business skillset and the privilege of my position could be used to help people.

But I was still disturbed by the lack of agency among these young people. That was true for both the boys and the girls, but somehow the girls had an additional challenge—that of lingering gender expectations. I often saw that the boys fought back, whereas the girls tended to be more conflicted about self-advocacy and power dynamics. Mental health challenges, particularly in the adolescent population, require staff with specialized skills to effect long-term change and wellbeing. When mental health intersects with poverty, addiction, racialization, or gender issues, the problems become even more complex to treat.

When I spoke to my superiors about this at the board office, I was told that I was not a social worker and that my job was to facilitate teaching and learning. And although we had resource staff available through the board to work with young people in need, there simply weren't enough of them to ably address all of the needs, which were so overwhelming. These heartbreaking stories have stayed with me, and I have attempted to capture them in *Class Lessons.*

CLASS
LESSONS

Addy

Hell on wheels is how she was described. I looked at the girl in front of me and wondered what she had done to deserve such a description. The official diagnosis was ODD, with uncontrolled rages. Addy was sullen, oversized for her height, and was wearing leggings with holes. She had chalky white colouring and badly cut, bleached hair. Her rounded face was studded with multiple piercings over both eyebrows, the sides of her nose, her top and bottom lips, and her chin. Later, I would see the grouping of three spikes on her tongue. Threaded through her nostrils was a prominent steel ring.

Her stepfather asked to speak with me privately. I walked Addy to her first class and left her with an unfamiliar teacher and a room full of students she would not know. I returned to her stepfather who recounted her sad history, culminating in her out-of-control behaviour. I studied him while he spoke to me. He was sixty at least. His fingers were calloused and nicotine stained, his clothes worn but neatly pressed. He wore the local uniform of the nearby stamping plant, heavy poly-cotton pants and a shirt. His eyelids were droopy, shielding his eyes, and the set of his mouth was slightly recessed, making his yellowed teeth seem over-large.

I confess I didn't listen to his words as much as assess him. When he had finished his tale, which seemed well rehearsed, I asked my first question.

Why did you do it? What motivated you to take her?

He paused briefly.

She could have been mine. I knowed her ma for years. And nobody wanted her.

Was there no other family?

Her bitch of a ma was a whore and a crackhead. Families don't keep in touch with those types.

How did you manage her as an infant?

Me own mother helped out. She lived with us. She died eight, nine years ago. It's been the two of us since.

And has Addy always been this angry, this oppositional?

Ya, she's a right bitch. Just like her ma. I'd give her back if I could.

All fourteen-year-olds can be challenging whoever their parents are. What matters most is that they feel loved and cared for and that we hold them accountable for their actions and help them to learn from their mistakes.

My responses were prim and automatic, using words I repeated countless times to dozens of frustrated or despondent parents. The words expressed what I believed, and they typically helped to soothe their upset. But not this time. The man before me was unmoved and angry.

I do me best. But by fuck, she wrecks everything. I try to keep the place nice, but she won't even clean up after herself. Won't help with the dishes or the housework. Shuts herself in her room and fuckin' screams at me when I go near. She's sick in the head, that one.

Has she ever had counselling?

She went to the anger management at John Howard. Twice she took it. Didn't make any damn difference. She'll end up in jail for sure.

Well, how can I reach you Mr. Williams in case I need to speak with you again?

He gave me his cell number and left. I watched him walk away. As a matter of routine, I called Children's Aid. I verified his identity and the custodial arrangements. I tried to find out from the worker if there was an open file, but she wouldn't breach confidentiality. Having done what due diligence I could, I moved on to other matters.

I saw Addy at lunch the next day. She was standing by herself in an empty stretch of corridor. I smiled and attempted to engage her in conversation. She looked down at the floor and wouldn't make eye contact. I glided away and continued my supervision, leaving her pressed against the wall, drinking from a large two-litre bottle of cola. By day four, Addy had been sent to my office multiple times. She huddled in a corner chair, squeezing herself into a compressed knot. I tried to reason with her, to gently question her. I used a soft voice and asked open-ended questions. I simply tried to understand what was making her feel the need to curse and swear at her teachers and classmates. Gradually, as her visits became more numerous, she began to drop hints.

They were making fun of me. Said I was fat, and I smelled.

No one wants me in their group.

The teacher thinks I'm stupid.

I spoke to the staff and asked for their assistance. I changed all of her classes and put her in a less challenging academic program. Every day was the same. Four periods in the day meant she would be sent to the office four times. I began to wonder if she was enjoying the attention I was giving her. I set goals for her. Try to stay in class for at least fifteen minutes before losing her temper or becoming rude. Listen to the lesson before being kicked out.

I like your perfume, she said to me once, surprising me.

You smell like a mother should smell.

We high-fived each other if she made it through half the period before being sent out. I spoke to her teachers again. I asked if they would seat her outside the classroom door if she needed to be removed and not to the office. One day, she threw her desk, one of those clunky arrangements with the attached seat, halfway down the hallway shrieking, *no goddam fuckin' way* at her teacher.

I filled out a referral for the school psychologist. Mr. Williams came into the school to sign the paperwork. He was surprisingly ebullient.

Told ya' she was an ungrateful bitch, he said. *Won't do a fuckin' thing anyone asks.*

He somehow felt vindicated by her behaviour.

As an infant, Addy had been found mewing pitifully in a dark closet, dehydrated and covered in feces and flies. Her mother had been dead for several days and was found with maggots crawling on her body. The rooming house where they lived was her mother's place of business, and the baby was put in the closet when clients arrived. It was the smell of her mother's decaying body that alerted other residents to her death.

Addy liked the psychologist. I even saw a hint of a smile when she walked by my office after one of their sessions. We didn't talk about what was said during those appointments. But for a little while, at least, I thought we had found something that was helping. I continued to set goals for her in the classroom: stay for the lesson and then ask the teacher to work in the library or the special education room. Take control and leave the room before you blow up. I began to restrict her access to my office and deny her the corner chair where she liked to curl up and watch me work. When she was sent out of class in one of her rages, I attempted to make her sit outside my office until she calmed herself.

You're just like the rest, she screamed. *You don't give a shit about me! You hate me. I'm disgusting to you.*

I wanted to comfort her: to wrap her in my arms and soothe her but I couldn't. Instead, I saw myself hugging an exhausted weepy little boy, calming him until the crying was overtaken by fatigue, and holding him closely until his body relaxed, and he climbed up onto my lap. But she was not my son, and I needed to keep a professional distance. The situation troubled me deeply. I didn't understand how a fourteen-year-old girl could contain such rage. Her stepfather seemed well-intentioned. He was involved. There were kids here who would befriend her if she would let them and staff who would be kind if she gave them an opportunity.

I found myself worrying about her when I was at home in the evenings. At the dinner table, we took turns talking about our day and sharing important information. There wasn't a lot I could talk about in front of my son, but I remember once telling him a little about Addy. I didn't go into details or share her name, but I did tell him that I was worried about a girl who had lost her mother.

That's sad, responded my son. *Who will teach her girl stuff?*

One morning when I arrived at school, there was an irate message on my answering machine. Mr. Williams left word that Addy had destroyed the house the previous evening and he had finally kicked her out. According to the message, he was out playing darts with his friends and came home to discover that she had smashed every plate and glass in the house, thrown the television across the room, and emptied the fridge by tossing the contents on the kitchen floor. They fought, and he had locked her out. His message was heated and colourfully punctuated with his usual expletives and profanity.

Worried about where Addy had spent the night, I was anxious to ensure her safety. I stood outside the front doors of the school to watch for her. When she arrived, I ushered her into my office. She went straight to the corner chair, and I saw she was fighting back tears. I went to the fridge and returned with food and a juice box. I was relieved to see her accept it.

What happened last night?

Nuthin'.

Where did you sleep?

In the park. Under the bushes.

You must have been cold.

It was better than stayin' in that shithole.

I've been by your house. It doesn't look like a shi-hole to me.

He's a fuckin' asshole. He hit me.

Where? Show me.

She lifted her head and turned her face towards me. I saw the beginnings of a large bruise on the side of her face.

I'm going to have to call Children's Aid. No one should hit you, ever. No matter what you've done. And I can't have you sleeping in the park. It's not safe.

Good. Tell them I'm not going back. He's a fuckin' whack job.

Are you sure about that Addy? He's been awfully good to you.

You don't know shit about it. He just puts on this act, so everybody thinks he's some kind of goddamn hero. He's a fuckin' piece of shit. I goddamn hate him.

Her vehemence surprised me. Tears were now running down her face. She went to wipe at them with a sleeve, and I glimpsed something I hadn't noticed before: a raw wound just above her wrist. I reached for her arm and gently pushed the fabric up. She let me touch her. A series of straight scars ran up her arm. Some looked fresh.

I was horrified by the rawness of the wounds. They reinforced for me the urgency of getting her help.

Does anyone know about this, Addy?

She shook her head and pulled the material down to cover the marks.

Did you tell the psychologist?

She shook her head again.

Are the cuts just on your arms?

She shook her head.

Legs?

She nodded.

Anywhere else?

She touched her stomach.

Oh, Addy... why? Why do you do this?

I want to go to a group home. Away from my shit life. I'm not going back. I'll fuckin' kill him if he touches me again.

Has he hurt you before?

All the time.

I will call your psychologist and ask her to come, and then I will call Children's Aid. We'll work something out. In the meantime, I will take you to the library, and you can sit there and read a book and wait for me. Does that work?

No one can convince me to go back to that asshole. Don't even fuckin' try.

I won't, Addy. I promise.

By the end of the morning, the psychologist, the Children's Aid case worker, and the police had arrived at the school. They conferred with Addy behind closed doors. When they came out, they told me that her worker was taking her to the hospital and would then be placing her in a group home. The police officer stayed behind and spoke with me briefly.

It was her shit of a stepfather. I'm going there now to arrest him. He's been pimping her out and sexually abusing her. She says it's gone on weekly all her life. Her worker and the psychologist both believe her.

As soon as I heard the explanation, her rage and the cutting made sense. I was upset to know that I had missed it; that I hadn't suspected someone was hurting her. Her worker called me the next morning to say that Addy would not return to school for a few days. She told me that it was one of the worst cases of abuse she had ever encountered. An examination at the hospital had confirmed Addy's story. Two weeks passed with no new information and no sign of Addy. I finally received a call to say that Addy was being moved to a group home outside of the community to distance her from her stepfather. She had expressed the desire to see me before she was moved.

I helped empty the contents of her locker and gave her a bag for her school supplies. I collected her textbooks and walked with her back to the office. We didn't talk about what had happened. It was an awkward parting.

I could write, if you wanted, and say hey, and let you know if the kids in my new school are assholes.

I'd like that. I'd like that a lot, Addy.

Alright then. I will.

I didn't receive a letter from her, but I sent a parcel to her new group home in time for Christmas. I hoped that there was an approachable female counsellor there who would help her heal and teach her the sorts of things my son referred to as *girl stuff*. I bought her a soft woollen scarf and hat, thinking the colour would suit her. I packaged it with candy canes and a card. It bounced back in the mail a month later. I immediately called Children's Aid to ask if she was alright. Her group home was in another district, and my contact had to call there for an update. A couple of days later she phoned me back and told me that Addy had run away from the group home and was missing. Despite the best efforts of a caring team of professionals, Addy had disappeared. Hers is one of the faces I still look for in a crowd.

Starr

The strobe lights were the first clue that I should have turned away. Instead, I grasped the pitted brass handle and pulled the door outwards. Four teenage girls filed solemnly past me while I held it open. They were dressed in their finery. Hair combed neatly, lip gloss applied, heavy eye makeup. All of them wore short little dresses with high-heeled sandals. They toppled and swayed slightly as they navigated the dimly lit hallway. I watched them protectively while scanning the grotty walls and eying the soiled carpet. The flashing lights continued, blinding me every few seconds with their pulsating flares.

Heavy metal music was blaring through the speakers, and the large room we had entered was shuddering with distorted guitar shrieks, smashing drums, and screaming vocals. Using only the intermittent flashes as a guide, I found seats for the girls and gestured for them to stay there until I returned. In another flare of light, I saw how frightened they looked.

I stumbled through the tightly packed throng. As my eyes adjusted to the spasms of light, I sought the one girl we had come to connect with. Shoulders pushed against me as I was pressed against bodies. I saw that some individuals were gyrating, fists raised in the air, while others were huddled in small groups, embracing. The smooth buttery feel of leather brushed my skin. The smell of something strong and musky, a sickening cat piss odour, filled the room. Dry ice was smoking, and drifts of fog further impeded my vision.

Just then, a hand gripped my arm tightly. I looked up and saw a figure glowering at me. He was tall and wide and clad entirely in black leather. Our eyes locked in one of the brief explosions of light. Despite my alarm, I had a function to perform. I took a deep breath and shouted at him.

I need to see Starr. I came from the school.

To my relief, he nodded and began to push a way through the crowd. *Out of the way,* he shouted, *this here's Starr's teacher.*

She was standing near a wall surrounded by a group of adults. A tall woman stood near her, petting her hair protectively. Starr saw me at once and stepped forwards.

You came? she mouthed.

Her face was swollen by tears and no sleep.

Of course. I brought your friends.

We hugged briefly, and she took me by the hand and led me to her mother. The crowd separated as she pulled me towards a small dais. A white coffin was positioned on a table. There was a long line in front of the area. We waited while a woman moved towards the coffin with her legs spread, and arms held out straight to her sides. Suddenly she jerked into action, tearing something from the sleeve of her jacket and tossing it into the coffin. I watched as a couple of men led her away, and a second person approached, a man this time, to repeat the same strange ritual.

Starr tugged on my hand and pulled me closer.

This is my mother, she said. *Isn't she lovely?* I stared at the figure lying at rest. Barely thirty, I thought, and gone well before her time. I understood that the ruptured aneurysm had been sudden. Her straight blonde hair streamed out from under a tight-fitting leather cap. Her face had been painted with heavy foundation and black lipstick. She wore a black leather vest for a top. The rest of her body was softly mounded with torn patches like eerie rose petals, filling the coffin. Loose threads still clung to their edges.

She's beautiful, I shouted.

Strong hands gripped my shoulders, and I was physically steered away so that others in the queue could come forward. I watched in the brief flames of light, as mourners approached and contributed their torn patches to the pile. Stumbling again, I made my way back to the girls. They were sombre. I smiled confidently in an effort to reassure them. Leaning close, I indicated that we would leave as soon as the service was over. They were to file out the way we came in and not speak to anyone.

If we get separated, I hollered, *wait for me at the car.*

They nodded.

Finally, the music was turned down, and a single spotlight illuminated a microphone stand. The beam of light illuminated a corner of a heating vent, and I saw the outline of a camera lens behind it, just a momentary glimpse. We were being filmed. An elderly man, stooped and with a limp, emerged from the darkness and made his way into the circle of light. He wore a shark-skin suit with a dark turtleneck. His voice was raspy, his face heavily scarred and pock-marked. The room quieted, and he talked about family and the larger family everyone also belonged to. He mentioned Starr's mother and called her *the mother to all, taken before her time.* He said she would ride again and we should all ride proudly, knowing she was in a good place. He pledged to look after her daughter. And that was it. No hymns, prayers, or poems. The music was cranked up, the strobe reactivated, and the funeral service ended.

I signalled to the girls that it was time to leave. They stood and pushed ahead eagerly. I made to follow them but was abruptly stopped. Hands reached out to me. I was embraced and thanked for coming. I recognized parents and local shop owners. All of them were in biker leather with large insignia emblazoned across chests, backs, and arms. Men that I did not know had tiny tears tattooed on their faces, one with as many as four. Blue-inked tear drops on weathered faces.

Breaking away, I rushed to the girls, getting them inside the car with the doors locked quickly. I was breathing hard. I couldn't get out of the parking lot. Black Harleys were everywhere, clogging the exits. Lines of long, battered limos snaked through the driveway. Mine was the only vehicle not black—a pristine little Ford in shiny silver, which seemed frivolous amid the mourning. I watched while the coffin was carried into the hearse and the rear door closed. It pulled out of the curved driveway and was immediately flanked by Harleys. Within seconds, the convoy had merged onto the main road and had driven away. The throaty roaring of what must have been two hundred bikes continued to sound even as we drove in the opposite direction.

My passengers were quiet. I glanced in the mirror and saw them clinging to one another. Large eyes looked back at me. I tried to reassure them by telling them that Starr would be well looked after. I could smell the dull stink of fear, an acrid stench.

When I pulled into the school parking lot the next morning, I saw three bikers parked beside my numbered space. I pulled in and turned off the ignition. I reached for my bags and stepped out of the car. I held the key fob tightly in my right hand, my fingers poised on the alarm. I took a step towards the building.

Mornin' Miss. Doan mean to bother ya' but we been waitin'. We saw ya' at the funeral. Can ya' talk to us?

They knew me. Knew which parking spot was mine. Knew I was the vice-principal. Starr must have told them. They probably even knew that she'd cried in my office two weeks ago after a fight with her boyfriend. I glanced up at the three burly men. All wore helmets, and their biker insignia was in full view. Their Harleys were big enough to plow me down. I was in real fear of these men. I knew they ran all of the prostitution and drug trafficking in the area. I was trembling but I nodded at them.

Come inside.

At least the security cameras would have a picture of my killers. I thought of my small son and husband as I unlocked the door to the main office. I briefly wondered if I would ever see them again.

They followed me inside. I smelled their leather and something else. Weed, maybe, or cigars. I couldn't tell. I led them to my office and unlocked the door with shaking hands. Maybe the board would name a school after me if I were killed in my office. I knew I needed to focus, stay calm, and not panic. I sat down and used my prim voice, the one I used when chewing out a student.

What can I do for you gentlemen?

It's about Starr. We doan know who her old man is. Her mom, God rest her, said she never knew for sure who the father was. It dint matter. Starr's grandparents want her. We doan know what's best. We came here because ye showed respect. We figured ye could tell us what's right.

I sat at my desk, dumbstruck for a moment, absorbing their words. Relieved to know that they weren't going to kill me, I glanced at their hands. No visible weapons. I stammered my response.

I don't know the answer. Not right now anyway. Will you let me phone Children's Aid and consult with a lawyer? If you come back tomorrow morning at the same time, I will tell you what the authorities say. In the meantime, where is Starr?

With us. Sharon's taking good care of her. She's her mother's best friend. Starr's known her forever.

I nodded.

Come back in the morning. Invite her grandparents and bring Starr. I'll try to help.

They thanked me like a group of young boys on their best behaviour and left my office. I heard their bikes roaring away a moment later. A flush of adrenaline coursed through me. My hands were trembling. I sat there until my colleagues began to arrive, and I then forced myself to move. The day was spent retelling the story and consulting with authorities. People offered to sit with me the following morning, but I was afraid of making my visitors uneasy. If they were going to kill me, they had already had their chance.

The next morning, nine bikes and one car were waiting for me at the school. The car was a rusted old Buick with a sagging rear bumper. An older couple were sitting inside. I motioned to everyone to follow me, and we solemnly walked into the building. Starr was not with the group. Inside the office, they all began to talk at once. Competing claims. Animated arguing. Shouting. I silenced them with my hand and an impatient *Be quiet or get out!*

They looked surprised.

I continued.

Everyone will get their say. But in turn. First, I want to know where Starr is.

She's coming later.

Okay. Good. I need to see her. I will tell you what I found out. According to the authorities, custody of Starr reverts to any living blood relative. And if we don't know who her father is, then that means her grandparents become her guardians.

What the fuck?!

They don't know shit about her!

We raised her.

That's not what her mother, Val, would have wanted.

We want to adopt her.

The group began to talk all at once. Again, I had to silence them.

I need to hear from her grandparents.

Her grandmother spoke up. I was surprised by the strength in her voice, belying her timid, thin figure in a pink cardigan.

Our daughter, Valerie, she lived rough. Made choices we didn't agree with. Got mixed up with this lot. We tried our best. But the drugs and the parties, they drew her back. She came home from time to time. She knew we loved her. But she always left again. We locked her out, finally. Said we had enough. We want to keep Starr safe from all of this. We'll give her a good home.

She looked around the room defiantly when she was done, daring anyone to question or challenge her. The room was silent. They were taking her in, measuring her words. Finally, a woman at the back shouted.

We helped raise her. We love her. We're what her mother wanted!

The words hung in the air. The vehemence with which they were uttered had changed the tone of the room. I felt my knees quaking under the desk. It would be easy, I thought, easy for this to escalate. I wondered if the police were undercover nearby. This crowd probably carried knives.

We need Starr, I said. *I need to see her.*

Low voices began to murmur. There were hurried conversations. I waited.

A woman at the back of the room left and returned a couple of minutes later leading Starr by the arm. I was relieved to see her. She looked pouty and defiant. There was nothing timid or frightened in her demeanour. No visible signs of tears. I spoke softly.

Starr, do you know why we're all here?

Yes.

Everyone in this room cares for you. Your mother's friends and your grandparents all love you. We have been talking about who should look after you. You are only fourteen. I have checked with Children's Aid and a lawyer. They both told me that your grandparents should become your legal guardians. Do you know your grandparents? How would you feel about living with them?

I want to stay with my mother's friends. They're my real family.

I'm afraid you're not old enough to make that decision yet, Starr. How would you feel about living with your grandparents if they agreed that your mother's friends could visit and spend time with you?

She looked around the room wildly, seeking direction from the group. A few of the bikers protested.

What if she lives with us and we let her visit Val's folks?

No, that's not what Children's Aid said. She needs a stable home environment. She needs to attend school.

I looked at Starr. Her head was down, and she was staring at the floor. Slowly, she looked up.

I guess. If that's what I have to.

Her grandparents smiled, and they both reached across to embrace her. She shook them off.

Thank you for coming, I said. Thank you all for caring so much for Starr during this terrible time. Thank you for trusting me. Starr, I know that your grandparents will do the very best they can to love and support you. I'll see you at school next week, okay?

She nodded. Sullen. I glanced at her grandparents. They were hovering over her. Ebullient. They thanked me briefly and pushed her through the crowd to the doorway. Starr was hugged and touched and kissed. The bikers thanked me respectfully, and with old-fashioned courtesy, they bowed their heads in barely perceptible nods before leaving my office.

I sat there and listened for the sound of the bikes as they left the parking lot. I had survived. Starr was with her biological family. All was returning to right—as right as the situation could be when a fourteen-year-old girl was left without her mother. But Starr didn't return to school. Her grandparents called me a couple of days later and told me that they had taken her home and showed her the bedroom that was to be hers. They had eaten dinner, watched television, and gone to bed. In the morning, she was gone. The hydro and phone lines had been cut in the night. They hadn't heard a thing. They walked half a mile to the nearest house to call for help. The police told the grandparents what they already knew: There was no point looking for her. The bikers had made their own decision. Although I knew she was loved, I despaired to think of the life she would have.

The South End

*F*uck *you, you fuckin' crusty fucker.* An eloquence of fucks. Adjective. Verb. Noun. There was an English lesson in there somewhere. She was fifteen and suspended from school. Irony.

Her teacher was, according to Summer, *a fuckin' perv,* but the real reason for skipping was a shift change. At 3:00 p.m., the lines formed at the east gate, past the wooden security shack and the twelve-foot-high fencing with barbed wire. The line snaked back, curled around the plant, engines running, while the short-of-breath security guard, in a grey Stainmaster shirt and pants, checked the truck beds and trunks, searching for stolen bumpers and hand tools. The line could take forty-five minutes to clear.

They're all fuck'in pervs. They like it when I jump in and show them my tits. For a twenty, I go down on them, and they don't lose their place. I pull my hair back. They like that. Short skirts and t-shirts with no bra. Makes 'em hard. I can do five in a row, easy. Then I puke it up. Bet you can't make no fuckin' hundred bucks in half an hour.

She was in grade nine. I was shocked to discover that thirty minutes from my safe, middle-class home people lived in impoverished circumstances. No hydro. No water. Whole families squatted in abandoned buildings. Street kids slept in wrecked cars. Young people arrived at school in deep winter without coats or boots, sitting at their desks with bleeding gums and teeth loose from scurvy.

Summer was a survivor. She had already found a way to look after herself. The monthly cheque her mother received paid the rent and a few bills. There was never enough left for a full month of food. It was her mother who had sent Summer to "work." Told her where to find the men and what to say to them. How to swallow.

Summer and I had one standoff. I had attempted to chastise her for not making school a priority.

Fuck you, bitch, she snapped.

Her blue eyes focussed on me intently. She moved her tiny childlike body right up to me, placing her feet apart in a firm stance. She clenched her small fists and spat at me.

You just don't fuckin' get it!

We would have looked ridiculous to a passerby: me, the authority, dressed in a flowered summer dress, stepping backwards from the girl, who was all of ninety pounds, looking menacing and ready to pounce.

She left school in early October. I was patrolling the smoking area at lunch when a battered black limousine pulled up, recruiting workers to harvest pot up north. She seemed to be expecting the summons and jumped in without hesitation. She called to a couple of others, and they climbed in as well.

See you in two weeks, one of them cheerfully called out while pulling the door shut.

I tried to get the license plate number, but it was covered with tape.

We attempted to call the girls' homes, but the phone numbers were out of service and the addresses bogus. It was not uncommon to discover that many of our students listed the local convenience store as their mailing address. We notified the police department, but in truth, no crime had been committed. They were not missing. They were "employed." This was not, I was told, an atypical disappearance.

There was a biker clubhouse to the east of us, and when they were having a membership meeting, they would swing by the school and collect a dozen girls, offering them free modelling lessons. Drugged and costumed, the girls would be used as dancers and live entertainment. The lucky ones might make it back a week later. Others, more susceptible to the crack-laced pot, would develop an affinity for the drug that would hold them captive.

Some of the girls told Jade this when they returned and she, in turn, told me. Jade was fifteen and had decided that I could be trusted. She often dropped by my office to give me a heads-up on something important.

The guys in the black limo, Miss, are messed. They're all fuckin' whacked. They don't give two shits about nobody. They all got fuckin' tats from prison. Tears for every sonofabitch they killed. Two or three each. And tattooed shit crawling up their necks. They're fuckin' psycho. There are girls locked in rooms in the basement. You gotta' tell people to stay away from that limo.

Jade was my source. If something was about to go down anywhere in the school, she would let me know. It wasn't that she particularly expected me to do anything about it; she just wanted me to know that she was connected. I respected this. Jade aspired to dance at the Dino, a local hang-out for guys on the line, where sixteen-year-old girls could jump on a table and earn whatever money was shoved into their costumes. The costumes themselves didn't have to be fancy—laced leather skirts, bikini tops, and strappy heels would do. Sometimes the girls wore their outfits to school and were indignant when I made them cover up with a t-shirt.

I tried to tell Jade that there was more to life. That she could go to college and work anywhere she wanted. She scoffed. College was not part of her world. She was vociferous in her contempt for my rule-ordered sanctimony. She showed me her tracks and the tiny puncture marks between her toes. I learned to abbreviate my lectures, curtail my judgment, and laugh a little.

K, Miss, like what the fuck do I need to know that shit for? Ya' think some Joe's gonna come up to me and say, "Yo, Jade, like can you show me how to fuckin' calculate the circumference of a cylinder"? No way, Miss. It's just a bunch of fuckin' useless bullshit.

Although she was only fifteen, she had things to do, places to go, money to earn. If she dropped by the school three or four times a week, attending two or three classes a day, that was a concession. A good-faith demonstration that conceded a willingness to credit that maybe there was something to learn. As long as we didn't *just fuckin' waste her time.*

One afternoon, as the bell rang, our doors were pushed open, and streams of teenagers escaped from the building, running purposefully to the front field. A car pulled up, and a young man I did not know jumped out with a length of pipe in one hand and a knife in the other. I ran towards the crowd that was quickly forming. They broke apart respectfully when I reached them, and I stepped into the ring. One of our students, a grade ten boy, lay in the grass curled into a fetal position; his arm was slashed and his face and head were badly beaten. The attacker escaped in the waiting car. The boy was in shock. I radioed the office for an ambulance. The onlookers stood back, watching me.

What happened? I screamed at them. *Who did this? Tell me what just happened here!*

But they were quiet and avoided eye contact with me. The victim couldn't or wouldn't speak either.

Is this what you want? I yelled. *Do you want this violence at school? Tell me what happened!*

They stepped backwards, away from my anger, and the crowd thinned quickly, leaving me alone in the centre of the field with the wounded boy.

A couple of days later, Jade dropped by my office.

It was a set-up, Miss. A beating-in. He had to prove himself.

I was incredulous.

You mean he knew the attackers? He could have been killed.

Yeah, sure. But now he's safe. He belongs. He made it to the first level. He's protected now.

What do you mean, the first level? What gang is this?

I'm not sayin'. Miss, there's some shit you shouldn't know.

Why not?

Cause they're fuckin' all over, that's why. And they'd mess me up if they thought I was talkin' smack about them.

What's the first level? What does that mean?

It's like beginner. To work your way up, you gotta' do shit. Bad shit. And then you move up.

What kind of bad shit, Jade?

You know, small stuff. Rob a store. Steal a car.

And then what happens?

Then, you become trusted. More powerful. Then you have to gangbang a chick. And the last thing is you whack someone. That's all I know.

I was silent. And she was scared. Just telling me these things had subdued her.

Ya' gotta' be careful, Miss. There's a lot you don't know. You can't mess with this shit.

I took in her message and knew she was telling me the truth. I worried about her though and could not help but wonder what she would be like if she attended another school and lived in another community. At fifteen, she was lovely but dressed like the tough, south-end chick she was. Her hair was shoulder length and carefully curled into soft, big waves. She wore thick foundation with elaborate eye makeup, intense red lip gloss, and glitter on her cheekbones. Tight jeans and a deeply unbuttoned, sheer black blouse comprised her look. It suited her. But sometimes, I just wanted to scrub her face to see what she looked like underneath the layers of paint. It suited her. I wondered what it would take to get her to college.

You can be so much more than this, I had repeatedly told all of them. *You can be anything you want to be.*

Hey Miss, Jade beckoned to me one day in the hallway. *I met this really cool guy. He's gonna look after me.*

I don't remember my exact response, but it was likely something prudish and unenthusiastic, like, *well I hope he wants you to graduate.*

This is it! she announced about a month later.

She had dropped into my office and was perched on the edge of my desk.

You'll be glad to know, I'm fuckin' done. Checkin' out. Gonna have a kid. You're not gonna have to mess with me no more.

A baby? I repeated stupidly. *Are you getting married, Jade?*

Fuck, no! I'm gonna be a baby momma. He don't gotta' marry me for that.

But Jade, I protested, *you're so smart. You could do so much with your life.*

An' I'm doin' it, bitch. Don't you see? It's workin' out. I'm gonna' have my own kid. I get paid to have kids. Lots of be-oot-tiffal babies.

My protests and sadness were left unspoken. Instead, I looked at her. She was smiling at me, looking happy and confident. This was something she could do. It was something that made sense to her. She lived in a world that I could only glimpse.

Deanna

Deanna believed that she was a Celtic goddess. She claimed to belong to a group of women who called themselves Sisters of the Moon. It was a real thing, and the girls only met on full-moon nights in a secret location. It sounded as if it might be on the flats down by the car plant, outside the security fencing. It was private and forbidden land, deemed particularly unsafe as the ground was marshy and potentially treacherous. This was the first lengthy conversation I had ever had with Deanna.

I tried to believe her, but the group's name sounded suspiciously like the title of an old Fleetwood Mac song. Although I was skeptical, I studied her while she spoke to me and tried to look as though I was taking the story seriously. She had clear, lightly freckled skin, violet eyes with long eyelashes, and straight blonde hair pulled back tightly in a ponytail. She was only sixteen, and there was an openness to her expression that was quite endearing even though it was still childlike. I wondered why she had dropped into my office, apropos of nothing, to tell me this strange tale. She sounded quite sincere. I thanked her for coming and sent her to class, not wishing to prolong a conversation that was so obviously an fabrication.

Deanna was in grade ten and had been an average student, easily blending into the fabric of the school. She was pleasant, polite, and socialized with a pleasant friend group. She hadn't distinguished herself in any discernable way until that morning. Her visit to my office was unprecedented. Several days later, I noticed her hanging around the staff room door at lunchtime. I approached.

You okay, dear? Do you need to speak with one of your teachers?

She smiled at me brightly.

I need to speak to Miss Burton about my project. I need help.

Just a minute and I'll see if she's available.

Miss Burton popped her head out of the door at my request and spoke with Deanna briefly. A day or so later, the situation repeated itself.

Oh-oh, I thought, this project must be challenging. Again, at my request, Miss Burton came out of the staff room and spoke with Deanna.

Days later, I saw Deanna once more, slumped on the floor outside the door of a staff workroom.

Hi Deanna, what's up?

I need to see Miss Burton, but she said she's busy and will see me in class. I really, really need her.

Just a sec. Let me check.

I entered the workroom and saw Miss Burton, chatting casually with her colleagues, a stack of marking in front of her on the desk.

Deanna's outside again, I said.

Deanna is always outside. I swear that girl is turning into a stalker.

She says she's having trouble with a project.

Her project is fine. That's just today's excuse. I've already given her a lot of extra help.

She just wants more personal attention. She's getting clingy.

Okay, then. I'll tell her you're marking.

I went back outside and told Deanna that Miss Burton needed to complete her marking. Deanna's eyes filled with tears.

I understand. She doesn't want to help me anymore.

No, honey. That's not it. Honest. But she has some other things to do. She'll see you in class today.

Thank you for trying.

A very sad and discouraged Deanna stood up and prepared to leave.

Would you like me to see if I can help you, Deanna?

She turned around and beamed a sudden smile at me.

Yes! That would be great! Thank you! I'll find you later.

She bounced away looking much happier.

Problem solved, I thought, smiling to myself.

Deanna received permission to leave class in the afternoon and came to see me for extra help. When I asked to see what she was working on, she slowly pulled a messy sheaf of papers from her backpack. There was no semblance of order to the accumulation, and I began to sift through them, smoothing the pages and sorting them into piles. This was a familiar task, as my elementary-age son had no sense of organization and randomly collected loose papers and handouts that he dealt with by simply scrunching them into his backpack. Remembering this, I smiled while I completed the routine task. When I was done, I asked Deanna to show me what she needed help with. She rummaged through the crumpled pages, finally extracting a now flattened but much-folded worksheet on the human reproductive system.

I don't know how to fill this out. She sighed. *I don't know what any of these words mean.*

Although she expressed innocence, there was something about her demeanour that seemed just a little bit off. She was too wide-eyed maybe or perhaps just a tad too helpless. My spidey senses were tingling. I felt like she was overplaying her hand, but I wasn't sure that I knew what the game was. With my alerts on high, I walked her through the assignment and sent her back to class as quickly as I could. I attributed her behaviour to simple attention seeking.

On a Monday morning not long afterwards, I had a visit from Miss Burton. She was clearly distraught and asked permission to close the door for a confidential chat.

I have to talk to you about Deanna, she began. *She showed up at my apartment on Saturday night.*

What?!

Yeah! At ten o'clock at night, the buzzer rang, and it was Deanna. I let her in and asked what she was doing at my apartment. She was carrying a small suitcase. She told me that she'd left home and needed a place to spend the night. I asked her how she knew where I lived, and she told me she had followed me home one night. But that doesn't make sense because I drive to work, and she would have had to take like three buses to get to my place, so I just don't understand that part. I told her she couldn't stay, and she started to cry and said she had nowhere else to go. I finally made her give me her parents' phone number, and I called them to say I was driving her home. But it was really upsetting. She's always trying to get in the workroom to sit beside me and do her homework during my prep. I let her do it once or twice, and now I'm sorry I ever started it. She's constantly hounding me.

It's a boundary issue. And it sounds like you handled it very well. I'm glad you drove her home. I will speak to her about boundaries. Would you like to be present for the talk?

Yes. I should hear what she has to say.

After the morning announcements, I got coverage for Miss Burton's class and arranged to have Deanna sent to my office. She arrived shortly, a little breathless from hurrying. She smiled at me brightly, but her expression changed rapidly when she saw Miss Burton sitting in an armchair.

Deanna, I began, I need to talk to you about boundaries. I understand that you showed up at Miss Burton's home on the weekend without an invitation. Teachers need their privacy, Deanna. It was wrong of you to intrude on Miss Burton's private time at home.

I thought she would want to know I was homeless. I thought she cared about me.

But you aren't homeless, Deanna. She drove you home.

Deanna burst into tears and began to sob in a credible outpouring.

You don't know what I put up with. My mother is mean to me. She abuses me. I can't tell you how bad it is.

I looked at Miss Burton to see what she thought of the story. Her face was soft and filled with compassion. Gone was her indignation at the breach of privacy, and instead what I saw was a teacher softening, ready to reach out to comfort Deanna. She was leaning forwards with an arm outstretched, and I shook my head abruptly, indicating that she should sit back.

Tell me more, Deanna. What is going on at home? Why did you decide to leave?

Deanna composed herself by loudly blowing her nose and using a balled-up handful of tissues to wipe her face. She settled into her chair with a sort of wiggling, squirming motion and began to recount a quite horrific story.

It only happens when my father goes to work. She locks me in the basement until school starts, and she leaves the lights off so I'm in the dark.

Is that a punishment for something?

No! She does it every day. She says that I'm worthless and don't deserve a nice house. That's why she shuts me in the basement.

Have you told your father this?

No! He wouldn't believe me! He always listens to her!

Does anyone else know about this?

You're the first people I've told. I didn't think anyone would believe me.

How long has this been going on?

Since I started school. But only when my father is at work.

Is there anything else, Deanna? Anything that you haven't told us?

Yes. Sometimes she hurts me inside.

What do you mean, inside?

You know, between my legs, inside.

She pointed at her crotch when she said this.

And how does she do this, Deanna? Can you explain?

Deanna's expression throughout had been extremely flat. The tears had stopped, and she was sharing her story in an emotionless tone. The statements were issued as calmly as if she were reading a grocery list. There was no change in her body language or her facial expression.

She keeps a glass bottle in the basement, and she puts it inside me. She says she has to get me ready. I don't know what that means. But once the bottle broke, and it cut me, just a little. And she had to get a new bottle. I have cuts inside.

It sounded like the plot of a terrible movie. I didn't believe her, but I didn't disbelieve her either. It was very hard to know. In the end, I called the school social worker and asked her to attend the school, urgently. I needed some direction and was confident that the social worker would help me to identify some next steps. She arrived within the hour, listened to my summary, and then took Deanna aside to chat with her. They were together for a half hour or so, and then the social worker came out and asked me to phone Deanna's father.

I spoke to him on the phone.

Mr. Richards, I was wondering if you could possibly come to the school today. Deanna has been sharing some troubling stories with us, and I think it would be good if we all sat down together to figure out how to best respond.

Can my wife come instead? What kind of stories?

Actually, we really need you to come. The stories involve your wife. Deanna claims that she is being abused. It would be really helpful if you would come to the school and listen to her yourself. We need you to help us to understand what is going on in your daughter's life.

Mr. Richards arrived within the hour. He had driven straight from work and was dressed professionally in a suit and tie. He looked flustered, and I was genuinely sorry to have disrupted his day with such a distressing communication. I ushered everyone into my office. Deanna did a doubletake when she saw her father sitting at the boardroom table.

Hi Daddy, what are you doing here?

Deanna went up to him, curling an arm around his neck. Her voice was timid and childlike, meek and sweet.

Please sit down, Deanna, I said. *Your father is here because we're all worried about you. You've told us some distressing things, and I want you to share with your father what you shared with us this morning.*

I can't. I can't tell him. He won't believe me.

Deanna was showing signs of distress and had become flushed and blotchy. She seemed tremulous and unsure of herself. I couldn't tell if this was a performance or if she was genuinely distraught.

Sit down, Deanna. Shall I start?

No! I'll tell him myself. By myself. You all have to leave!

I looked around the room, and seeing no objections, I nodded and stood to leave the room. Miss Burton and the social worker followed me. We waited outside my office in a large foyer at the front of the school. All of us watched the door carefully, waiting. Eventually, after what seemed like an interminably long half-hour, the door opened, and a teary Deanna slunk by us on the way to her locker.

I have to get my coat was all she said as she passed by.

The three of us returned to my office, where Mr. Richards was sitting alone, his face in his hands.

Mr. Richards?

He looked up.

I apologize, he said.

I don't know what's got into her. She's been telling stories for years. They seem to get wilder all the time.

Is there any truth to any of them?

I don't think so.

So, she's not a practising Celtic goddess?

He looked up sharply.

What?

She doesn't belong to a group called Sisters of the Moon?

He shook his head, incredulously.

She told you that?

She did. She also said that your wife locks her in the basement when you're at work. And that she sexually abuses her with a glass bottle.

Oh my God. No! My wife adores her. Spoils her rotten. Treats her like a princess.

But Deanna ran away from home on Saturday night. She showed up at Miss Burton's apartment, unannounced and uninvited. Something must have happened.

She told us she was going to a sleepover at her friend Cathy's. We didn't think anything about it.

But weren't you concerned when Miss Burton called you?

Deanna told us the party was cancelled, and she didn't know what to do, so she wandered around with some friends and someone told her that Miss Burton lived nearby, and they looked up her address, and Deanna called her and asked for a ride home. Didn't she drive all the other girls home?

No. Just Deanna.

I don't know what to say. She likes attention. Always has. But she's too old to be telling these kinds of stories. What should I do?

The social worker interjected.

First, you need to take her to the hospital. You have to ask them to examine her for signs of sexual abuse. We need to ascertain that nobody has been hurting her physically. Once you know the answer to that question, we can proceed. Deanna's need for attention is something that has to be addressed. It could be a symptom of a more serious concern.

Mr. Richards called me several days later to assure me that his wife had strongly denied ever having done the things Deanna had accused her of. The hospital had put them in touch with a clinical psychiatrist who had diagnosed borderline personality disorder and was now working with the family on the development of a treatment plan.

I shared the information with the social worker who concurred that borderline personality disorder was a possible explanation for the behaviour. Deanna did not come back to school for a couple of weeks. I assumed that all was well and that there would be no further issues. When she returned, she assiduously avoided eye contact with Miss Burton or with me. She was quiet and withdrawn in class but otherwise seemed to be acting normally. A couple of days later, I was monitoring the halls and encountered her leaving the bathroom. She seemed particularly fierce as she approached me. She stood in front of me, her fists clenched tightly at her side.

It's true, you know, what I said. Even if you don't believe me.

She walked away and entered her classroom before I could respond. When I returned to my office, our school police liaison officer was waiting to touch base with me. I felt a little shaken by Deanna's intensity, and so I shared the story with him, including the encounter I had just had experienced.

I have some time, he said. *Let me swing by the house and talk to her mother.*

Relieved to have someone else looking into the situation, I busied myself with other concerns. The next afternoon, our liaison officer returned and motioned for me to head to my office. He sat down carefully, wedging himself into a chair while he adjusted his holster and the equipment attached to his belt and vest.

Here's the thing, he said by way of an opener. *I swung by Deanna's house. Her mother was home. She offered me a coffee, and I went in, and we talked about what happened. She told me the whole story. Showed me pictures of Deanna as a small girl. They were all over the house. And after a while, I asked if I could look around for a minute, and she said sure. So, I went into the kitchen and saw a basement door and went down the stairs for a quick look.*

He paused, and I waited for him to continue.

So, you're not gonna believe this: in the corner of the basement was a pile of blankets and there were empty Coke bottles lined up beside it. I didn't know what to make of it.

Do you think Deanna put those things there?

I don't know. But there's nothing I can do. Her mother seemed surprised when I asked her about it. She looked convincing. She had these big purple eyes and looked at me all bewildered. Deer in the headlights sort of look. All we can do is see if anything else happens.

I am uncertain about what really transpired in Deanna's life. Her vehement insistence that what she had told me was true, seemed plausible. The police officer's findings also made her story seem credible, but I also knew that she could have staged the area. I was assured that she was receiving ongoing clinical help from a team at the hospital. I don't know if she was perpetuating an elaborate ruse to implicate her mother or whether her mother had successfully manipulated all of us into believing Deanna was unstable. I also don't know if Deanna was a member of Sisters of the Moon or not, although I think it unlikely.

But I believe she was experiencing trauma—whether it was real or manufactured. I was so grateful for the experienced social worker, hospital staff, and police officer who had all come together to offer such an immediate and caring response.

Gemma

I'd never seen Doc Martins before. Our new student from the United Kingdom was wearing them. Bright red leather boots with thick black soles, yellow stitching, and black laces. When I first met sixteen-year-old Gemma, she had short blonde curly hair and was wearing dark eyeliner, black tights, a denim mini-skirt, and those ridiculous-looking boots. She was animated and seemed excited to be starting in a new school. She spoke with the softest of refined British accents. Her mother had registered her the day before, and today was Gemma's first day of class. I asked a guidance teacher to escort her to all of her classes and to introduce her to some nice students. It should have been a nonevent.

The rumours started immediately. By the end of the first day, the prevalent theory was that Gemma was an undercover narc. The ludicrousness of the story was not to be credited, and teachers did their level best to quash the buzz. I now believe we should have taken the gossip more seriously. Gemma had been immediately marked as "other," and some students saw her as a threat.

Gemma seemed unaware of the stir she was creating. A quietly confident girl, she was polite to staff and eager to catch up on the coursework she missed. None of the girls chose to befriend her, however. One day, I saw her eating lunch alone in a corner of the cafeteria, and I floated by her table while on supervision and casually checked in on her.

How are you doing, dear?

I'm alright, thank you, she replied brightly.

Are you missing your friends? This was an awfully big move for you.

We said we'd write each other. I expect to hear from them soon.

It must be a little lonely for you.

I have my little sister for company. She's ten. We do things together after school and at weekend.

Are you settled in your new house and unpacked?

We're waiting on a freight shipment from home. It has our winter things and household bits and bobs.

It will be good to have some familiar things when they arrive.

I expect so.

She had a positive attitude and seemed to accept her current situation with good grace. I assumed that things would settle down and she would gradually become integrated into the social fabric of the school.

During Gemma's second week, I saw her walking to school with one of the boys who lived near her. They had connected, and I was delighted to see she had a friend. Gemma had changed the clothes she wore to school, adopting the sloppy-pyjama-bottom-with-t-shirt wardrobe, which the girls currently favoured. She was trying hard to fit in, but unlike the girls who wore their outfits with loose-fitting Uggs, she continued to sport her Doc Martins. The contrast of her gauzy mass of soft curls with jammies and Doc Martins amused me, and I observed her with some admiration. She was trying to comply with the crowd while making her own statement.

Buildings filled with hundreds of teenagers develop a unique synergy. You can feel it hum or throb when you're among a large group of them. You notice it in the halls between classes, the cafeteria at lunchtime, and the gym at game time. There is a distinctive energy that communicates unease, excitement, or boredom.

A couple of grade eleven teachers mentioned that there was a new tension and sense of unease building. Their instincts about such things were always on the mark, and I knew enough to trust them. I scheduled a couple of extra lunch monitors and increased supervision before and after school. I hoped that an increased staff presence would keep things calm. Soon, a whisper went around the building that there was going to be a fight at lunch. A couple of staff members grabbed walkie-talkies and jumped in their cars to follow the torrent of students swarming down the street. I stayed behind to notify the police.

I'm told that staff and police arrived at the scene shortly after the beating. The mass of students packed tightly in a large circle made it easy for them to locate. The fight took place in the backyard of a house close to the school. Gemma had been invited to hang out with some grade eleven girls and had innocently accepted the invitation. When they reached their destination, the girls accused her of being a narc, threw her on the ground, and began to punch her. One of the assailants had dragged her across the ground by her hair while the others took turns kicking her. It was over quickly and when the police arrived, the crowd dispersed. Students and staff streamed back to the school and filled me in on the gruesome violence.

Much later that afternoon, once he had spoken with one of the emergency room doctors, the school liaison officer visited the school and inventoried the extent of Gemma's injuries for me: concussed, eight teeth broken or kicked out, jaw and orbital structure fractured, broken ribs, and severe bruising. But the most horrific was the last item: loosened areolar connective tissue. The officer had to explain this to me in layman's terms: Her scalp had been partially removed by the dragging. I was sickened by his words. Such cruelty seemed unfathomable.

I helped the officers interview the students at the fight. Some of them were helpful and provided names. It took almost two days to meet with them all, suspend them, and call their parents.

The whole time, I just wanted to scream: *Are you f-en kidding me? What gives you the right? Is this the kind of world you want? Is this what you think school should be?!*

Everyone who went to the fight was suspended. The phone calls home were confrontational. Parents questioned our ability to suspend students for something that happened off school property. When I detailed the extent of Gemma's injuries, most of them backed down. Not all. Some were aggressive. Those individuals were invited to meet with me and the police to discuss community safety and citizenship. The main perpetrators were arrested and charged.

Gemma remained in intensive care for several days. Only family members were permitted to visit. I learned from her mother that the family was returning to the United Kingdom so that Gemma could have the necessary reconstructive surgeries there. Her mother's voice was weary but carefully modulated. Despite her tired state, she clearly communicated what she thought of my school, students, and country. All I could offer were my sincerest apologies and ridiculous-sounding good wishes. Even as I uttered the words, I knew that they would not begin to touch the hurt. There would be no balm for the horrific act of violence her family had experienced. When I hung up the phone, I closed my eyes and pictured Gemma's sweet, confident smile, her complete lack of guile, and what was once the soft globe of pale, soft curls that had framed her face.

I remember standing by the front doors of the school at afternoon bell one day, watching the groups of students as they left the building. They were not discernably monstrous. They were simply teenagers seemingly untouched by the sense of territoriality that had destroyed an innocent girl.

Reza

It was the first day of my new assignment. I'd been a high school vice-principal for several years but had recently been transferred to a different school. The move was considered part of my career development, but I wasn't entirely sure what to expect. I met with some staff briefly on a quick walk-through the week before and dumped some personal things into my new office. During my brief orientation, I learned that the upper-middle-class neighbourhood was greying out, causing infilling and demographic shifts. I also learned that the nearby apartment towers had been repurposed to provide subsidized housing for new Canadians.

After dropping off my small son at daycare and watching while he struggled up the stairs, bent forwards under the weight of his too-heavy backpack, I headed towards my new placement. It was a thirty-minute drive, and with luck, I would arrive before 7:30 am. Early starts were important. I had to ensure that the supply teachers were confirmed and that no one else had called in sick. I've never been a morning person, so the morning routine of getting everyone ready and out of the door on time took its toll on my stress level. I was grateful for the time alone in the car to slowly get myself in the right headspace for the day. I had to complete a dozen important tasks before the morning bell, and I ran through the priorities in my head.

The principal impressed me as someone meticulous and no-nonsense. I suspected that I would need to work especially hard to impress him. I had a feeling that his take-no-prisoners approach applied to staff and students. Before school started, I began an early morning walk-through of the building. Moments later, I was paged back to the main office. I hurried back to find the principal struggling to restrain a young man flailing angrily and trying to push past him into an inner office. The principal indicated I was to comfort a distressed young woman in the office. The boy was shouting angrily in a language that I did not recognize. Circling the tussling figures, I slipped into the smaller room and locked the door behind me. I went to the dark-haired girl who was cowering on the floor and gently guided her up and onto a chair. Intermittent pounding on the door continued for several minutes before it stopped. When it was quiet, I addressed her.

What is your name?

There was the sound of snuffling and then I heard, *Reza,*

Tell me what happened, Reza. Who is that boy?

I spoke softly and gently, trying by my tone to calm and reassure her.

My brother... Ali.

Why is Ali angry?

He believes... I have... dishonoured... the family.

The words were faint and came haltingly. They were difficult for her to articulate.

Why does Ali believe that?

I pulled a second chair close to her and sat facing her, our knees touching.

He saw me smiling at a group of boys who greeted me. I did not speak to them. I lowered my head and walked by. Ali says that I encouraged them by smiling.

What did he do to you, Reza?

He slapped me and kicked me here.

She pointed to her pelvic area.

He called me a whore. When I go home, my father will also punish me.

She began to cry, shuddering and shaking terribly. I glanced at her while processing her response. She was petite and had finely shaped fingers. She was dressed in oversized jeans and a bulky sweater. Her face was partially obscured by a delicate pink hajib. Later I would learn that she and her brother were both new students. Their family had moved here from Vancouver and before that from the Middle East. The head of guidance told me that their father was a political dissident and had fled the country under threat of death. The family had experienced a great deal of trauma during their harrowing escape.

We were reluctant to call Reza and Ali's father, so the principal and I decided I should be the one to call her mother. The mother's English was fractured, and I struggled to make myself understood.

Hello, this is Ms. Black from the school... I am calling about Reza... The high school... I am the vice-principal at Reza's school... Hello? Yes? I am the vice-principal... I am calling about Reza.

Reza finally took the phone from me.

She'll come, Reza said, hanging up the phone.

She has to walk. It will take fifteen minutes.

I nodded.

Would you like some ice?

I filled two baggies with ice cubes and brought them to Reza. She placed both of them between her legs. Her mother arrived soon after, accompanied by a second woman. The secretary ushered them into the room. Both women were beautifully dressed in knee-length tunics, matching trousers, and head scarves. Reza's mother rushed towards her daughter and embraced her in a tight maternal clutch and soothed and patted her affectionately. Reza renewed her crying while clinging to her mother.

I explained to them that Reza was not in trouble but that we were worried about her safety. The woman who had been introduced to me as Reza's aunt asked after Ali, and I explained that he was in a separate office with the principal. She spoke to Reza's mother quickly and then to me again in English.

Please to not send him home now. We will take care of Reza, but Ali is a man, and he will not listen. He should not come home until his father and uncle are there also.

The women left with Reza, and the principal and I tag-teamed Ali. We explained that his treatment of Reza was considered assault in Canada and that we would be reporting this incident to the police. Ali would not make eye contact with us and listened only nominally when my male counterpart was speaking. Whenever I spoke, he scoffed and sneered at me. I found myself angered and found it difficult to maintain my composure. I was glad to let the principal take the lead cautioning him. We left Ali in the in-school suspension room while the two of us conferred.

It was obvious that Ali would need a timetable change, as it seemed clear that we could not trust him to be respectful with female teachers. We also needed to ensure he did not share any classes with his sister. Although they were not twins, they were born in the same year and had been placed in the same grade.

Reza did not return to school for several days. When she did come back, I saw that her brother was trailing her and was carefully watching her movements and interactions with others. This cannot continue, I thought. He may well observe her walking to and from school, but he cannot expect to supervise her movements in the building. When Reza reached the front doors, she turned and held both her hands up in the stop position. She shouted something in angry tones at her brother. He responded by striding forwards and striking her hard across the face. She gasped loudly. I stepped closer to Reza and stretched out my arm to protect her. Ali pushed past both of us and merged into the crowded hallway.

Are you alright?

Reza nodded her head, even as one hand covered the cheek where she had been hit.

He needs to stop, she said.

Father and Uncle have said. We are to become real Canadians. He cannot continue the old ways.

She was defiant.

You must let me know if he hurts you again.

She nodded and walked confidently towards the locker bay.

Although we were reluctant to interfere in family concerns, it mattered to both the principal and me that Reza felt safe at school. We kept an eye on her, at lunchtime in particular. Her brother had become friends with some boys also from the Middle East. They were a tightly-knit group and were often together. Ali's group watched Reza closely during the lunch hour. They would choose a seat near her in the cafeteria, follow her to the library, and pursue her when she went outside into the garden.

I suspected that they were discussing Reza and her friends in critical terms. I couldn't understand what they were saying, but I recognized the universal intonations. Whenever I passed near, they made a soft clicking noise with their tongues against the roof of their mouths. Their disrespect made my cheeks burn hot. I felt that their attempts to intimidate Reza were also an indictment of all the females in the building.

The buildings where Reza's family lived housed a number of our students and their families. They came from many parts of Asia, the Middle East, the Philippines, and the Caribbean. Stories sometimes reached the school of conflicts among the teenage boys who lived there. There were often quite violent fights necessitating police intervention and some of these conflicts began to spill over into the school. Ali and his friends were frequently involved.

Several days passed without incident. I was still trying to acclimatize myself to the new school environment. Although I was an experienced administrator, everything about the staff and the student body felt unfamiliar. I was anxious in the mornings for my day to begin. But first, as always, I needed to drop my son off at daycare. We practised his spelling list in the car. I had printed the words out on a piece of cardstock and tucked it behind the car's visor. It was a t-word list with ten words beginning with the letter t. When he was learning something new, we would always repeat the information in a sing-song rhythm, which helped him to learn. For the word "tomorrow," for example, T-O-M was sung quickly, O on its own, R-R in a staccato, and O-W in a lower register. After he got out of the car and went inside, I drove to school with his vocabulary list replaying like a soundtrack. And then the words of a partial quote came back to me from somewhere: tomorrow and tomorrow and tomorrow… creeps in. I couldn't remember where it was from and knew that the reference would niggle at me.

That day at the end of lunch, there was a ruckus in the parking lot. A circle of students were screaming and cheering. We rushed outside to see a fight with Ali drop-kicking another boy in a succession of Jackie Chan moves. Watching Ali spinning and kicking in a blur of violence felt surreal. The crowd dispersed when we came close, and Ali, panting heavily, finally stood still. A boy named Ismet lay in a bloodied heap on the tarmac. We called for an ambulance and the police.

When we reviewed the security cameras, we saw that Ali had initiated the fight, taking the victim on suddenly with a series of drop kicks and punches. Ali was clearly a highly trained fighter. Ismet was cowering and offered no resistance to the assault, attempting only to shield his head from the blows. After reviewing the video, the police charged Ali with assault with a weapon and took him away in handcuffs. His obvious expertise as a fighter was considered a weapon.

Reza came rushing up to me in the hallway a little later in the afternoon. She was flushed and had obviously been crying, her headscarf had fallen down around her shoulders but she hadn't bothered to adjust it. Breathlessly, she asked how Ismet was. I didn't have any information for her, as we were still waiting to hear back from the police.

Are you friends with Ismet?

She looked downwards modestly, avoiding my gaze.

He lives in my building.

Is that why Ali fought him?

Ali hates him because he is from across the border at home.

Does your father know you are friends with him?

No. My father wishes for me to have a fine education. He wishes Ali to become a doctor or an engineer. He plans for me to become a pharmacist or a nurse or a teacher. Ali's arrest will bring shame on the family.

Will it bring more shame than finding out that you are spending time with a boy?

She answered with a small smile.

Shame is shame. If you feel no shame, then people do whatever they wish. We strive to be people who have both shame and decency.

Her rather cryptic response stymied me. I was certain she had said something profound, but I could not then puzzle out her meaning. All my interactions with this family had stretched me in terms of understanding how best to be supportive. They were trying so hard to embrace a new life, but it was difficult, and Reza was so clearly caught between their two realities.

At home later in the evening, dinner and dishes done, everyone quietly in bed, I finally managed to look up the quotation" *Tomorrow, and tomorrow, and tomorrow, Creeps in this petty pace from day to day.* It was from William Shakespeare's *Macbeth.* How far away from my university studies was this world I was now working in. Nothing in my formal education had prepared me for this dynamic. I had left the corporate world hoping to be helpful, and now I saw how limited my own skillset was, further complicated by my privilege and lack of contextual experience.

Ali was eventually convicted and sent to a juvenile detention facility. He did not return to school. Ismet's family moved out of the area shortly after the fight. Reza continued at the school, and over her years there, I saw her develop self-confidence and maturity. She was part of a large friend group and learned to navigate easily between cultural divides. Despite this, prior to commencement, she informed me that she would not be able to attend if she was expected to shake hands with our male principal. I assured her that I would happily present her diploma. She beamed at me with gratitude and attended the ceremony later that evening with her parents and aunt and uncle. All of them were smiling proudly to celebrate her achievement.

A rather self-important school board trustee was part of the stage party. He frequently left his seat to add his congratulations to the graduates and to pose for pictures. Unfortunately, despite being asked to remain seated until invited to do otherwise, he attempted to embrace Reza when she won an academic award. She deftly sidestepped past him and rushed off the stage. There were still cultural divides that could not be crossed.

Katie

Despite the professional need to treat all students equally, there are sometimes individuals with whom you feel a special connection. Katie was one of those special someones for me. She was mouthy and feisty and had the worst case of potty mouth I have ever encountered. She was being raised by a single dad and his mother. Her father and I had each other's phone numbers on speed dial. He often called me for advice when she was being particularly difficult. I often called him with the news that she had sworn at a staff member and was spending the day in our in-school suspension room.

Katie had an independent spirit and did not take well to the bell-driven schedule of school. She was constantly late in the mornings. This was one of the many areas of tension between her and her father. He didn't want to leave her alone in the townhouse when he left for work, so her unwillingness to get out of bed often meant that he himself was running late. At school, the office staff would routinely give Katie a late slip with a reminder of her lunch-time detentions owing, and she would snap out a loud *FUCK YOU!* without a second's hesitation. The staff would then redirect her to my office, where I had endless conversations with her about the inappropriate use of language. Katie would eventually calm down and apologize, but not before I assigned her additional detentions.

Despite my many interventions with Katie about language, I never felt that her cursing was intended to be malicious or offensive but rather was more of a vocabulary explosion. I wrote new words on post-it notes for her in an attempt to enrich her command of language with more socially appropriate choices. I was at pains to teach her to use the new lexicon as expressions of frustration instead of the colourful alternatives she typically employed.

Pleased with my new strategy, I sent Katie off to class one morning with "Botheration!" written on the front cover of her binder and across the back of her hand. I encouraged her to work on substituting the new word whenever she felt inclined to use the f-word. I promised to cancel ten detentions if she could get through the day without being sent to the office for swearing.

Mid-morning Katie was back in my office.

What did you do?!

Katie grinned at me a little impishly. *I used your new fuckin' word and I still got fuckin' kicked out of that ass-wipe class.*

How exactly did you use the word, Katie?

You know what a shit-faced old cow Brownson is, and she was goddamn going on about this shitload of fuckin' work we have to do, and all the time, she's walking up and down the aisle like an asshole army sergeant. And I'm just minding my own fuckin' business, and suddenly she's standing the fuck in front of my desk, and she's screaming at me that I need to pay attention. And so, I stand up and I goddamn look her in the eye and I say, "You are a botheration!" and the bitch goddamn kicks me out anyway. Like what the fuck?! You told me it was a good word, and I still get fuckin' sent down here. I don't need this shit!

Katie! Enough! Stop!

It was all I could do not to laugh.

Well, you fuckin' asked!

She was indignant and clearly felt that she was the wronged party.

Katie spent the rest of the day in the in-school suspension room, but I cancelled ten detentions because she had at least tried to use a new word. I also personally apologized to her teacher with the sheepish explanation that I was endeavouring to expand Katie's word choices. Although my apology was accepted, it was quite clear that the staff member did not appreciate the enrichment exercise.

Between Katie's long-suffering grandmother, her often exasperated father, and one-hundred-plus detentions, we were gradually able to curb Katie's use of colourful language. It was still salty, but she learned to refrain from using the f-word, at least, when speaking directly to staff.

Less is more, and not everyone needs to know what you think all the time, were two of the mantras that I tried to reinforce with her.

Katie was active socially and had a large friend group. She often drifted between different groups of students and went out of her way to be kind to some of the less popular girls. At some point during the winter, Katie fell deeply in puppy love with a grade nine boy. They held hands and walked around the building together beaming happily. It was pleasant to see. And one of the positive offshoots was that Katie, in her excitement to see her boyfriend, began showing up to school on time.

In mid-spring, Katie suddenly resumed her late arrivals. It was an abrupt change, and I wondered why her routine had altered. Then, while doing smoking area supervision, I saw her boyfriend with another girl. They were draped around each other, and there was no mistaking their involvement. I chewed my lip thoughtfully and wondered if Katie was aware of the situation. A couple of days later, she arrived particularly late, almost near lunch-time, to sign in for her morning classes. She was sent to my office, and I noticed that she looked unwell and had dark circles under her eyes.

You're late again, Katie. Are you feeling well?

She shook her head.

You look a little pale. Are you eating properly?

She shook her head again.

Can you tell me what's going on?

No.

Do you need to see a doctor?

She sat down in a chair and crossed her arms over her midriff. She shook her head again. When I looked at her, I saw that she was crying. I assumed it was a straightforward case of heartbreak. I waited quietly to see if she would tell me more.

I'm pregnant....

Oh! I see... Does your boyfriend know?

I told the cocksucker, and, you know what, the shitbag asked me if it was his. Like who the hell else would it belong to? Such a fuckin' dickweed. I don't know why I ever let that asshole stick his ...

Sssh, Katie. Sssh. Stop now.

I sat beside her and put my arm around her shoulders. She continued to cry. In between the occasional sob, she muttered her familiar litany of expletives. When she stopped crying, I passed her some tissues so she could mop her face.

Does your father know?

Yes... he wants me to have a ... you know...

I nodded.

It's an option. But you have lots of options, Katie. Have you been to the doctor yet?

My grandma's taking me this week.

Good. The doctor can talk to you about all of your options.

I'm keeping it!

Well, that's a big decision.

She hugged her midriff more tightly.

Well, it's mine. So, it's my fuckin' decision to make.

If you say so. You might want to talk to your doctor about all of your options before you decide.

No goddamn way. Nobody's going to talk a bunch of shit and change my fuckin' mind.

Well, okay then. I'm glad you've made a decision. Will your father and grandmother help you?

She nodded.

Well, congratulations, Katie. Babies are happy news!

She nodded again, still hugging herself. *And that shift-faced bastard prick is not coming anywhere near the kid. I'm keeping her away from him.*

You think it's a girl?

It has to be. I don't want some jerkoff of a boy to look after.

What if the baby is a boy?

It's a girl. And I'm calling her Jenny. I think that's pretty.

It is. It's a really pretty name. But what if she's a he?

Katie shrugged her shoulders.

It won't matter.

Katie, do you know why you want to keep this baby?

It's mine. And it will be mine to love. Forever.

I checked in with her the following week to see how the doctor's appointment had gone.

My grandma was nice. She stayed with me the whole time. My father is a fuckin' douchebag though. He went to the ass-wipe's house and told his parents that the little cocksucker had to pay child support. He's having a fuckin' shit about how much crap I'm gonna need, and how we have to fuckin' change the shithole of a townhouse around so the baby's room is next to mine. Like, what the fuck? And I don't get why he has to be such a mean prick and be all up in my damn face about every fuckin' little thing. But he said he'd buy the crib and shit.

Gossip travels quickly in a school, and word of her pregnancy was soon public knowledge. Also rumbling through the school was the news that her former boyfriend was denying that the baby was his. I was pretty sure that Katie would explode when she heard what he was saying. In an attempt to pre-empt a public scene, I called her down to my office.

Have you heard what Ben is saying, Katie?

She looked down and nodded her head.

Are you okay?

Another nod.

Would you like to talk to someone? Someone in guidance or the school social worker?

A gentle headshake. I saw that tears were plopping down, but she would not look at me.

Katie, hon, can I do anything for you?

Another headshake. Her silence was worrying. When the lunch bell rang, she stood up and wiped her face and left my office. That afternoon, Ben's mother phoned me.

I've just heard from my neighbour that Katie went into my house at lunchtime and hasn't come out.

How did she get in?

Through the garage. All Ben's friends know how. I texted Ben, and he's in class, and he doesn't know why she's there.

Can you go check on her? Can your neighbour go?

Absolutely not. We don't want anything to do with that little slut.

What would you like me to do?

Get her out before I call the cops.

I think you should call them, actually. If she's trespassing.

Well, you're no help, are you! She hung up the phone.

A chill came over me, and I called 911. Suddenly, I was terrified for Katie. I spoke to Ben and asked him to come to his house with me. He refused but gave me permission to enter. I arrived before the police and entered via the garage. I found her upstairs in a room I presumed was Ben's. She had stripped off most of her clothes and was lying in his bed. I tried to wake her, but she was limp and very sleepy. I wrapped her in a blanket and cradled her until the emergency responders arrived.

She was a child having a baby and was overwhelmed by the sadness of a broken heart. I wept while I held her. They pumped her stomach out at the hospital. I can only imagine what she had to say to the nurses when she was in recovery. Later, I encouraged her to join a pregnant-teens program where she could continue her schooling while also learning the skills she would need to care for the baby. She visited me after Jenny was born, a tiny nugget of pure joy, swaddled in pink. Katie's face shone with pride even as she told me that *the kid has a fuckin' set of lungs and drives me Christ-crazy when she's bawling.*

Just like her mum, then, I said, hugging her lightly before she turned to leave.

Sidney

Our woodshop teacher decided to clear out his work space one day and sell off the unclaimed projects that were cluttering the classroom. We advertised the sale in our school newsletter, and I offered to keep a small inventory of the student-made shelves and plant stands in my office. They were made with pine and, at ten dollars each, would help to recoup the cost of the wood. I was in my office one afternoon when a secretary ushered someone down the hall to meet me who wanted to view the wooden offerings. It was a parent I hadn't met. She was exquisitely dressed, with a designer handbag, stilettos, huge sunglasses, hair pulled back in a sleek ponytail with a fat velvet bow, flashy rings, and chunky pearls. It was a very classic look, but she did the Anna Wintour thing and didn't remove her sunglasses indoors. I hate not being able to see someone's eyes when I'm talking to them, and dislike even more, looking at the distorted reflection of my own face in their lenses.

Our elegant parent didn't strike me as the crafty-type, someone who would enjoy painting or sanding little pine shelves, but she was enthusiastic about the quality of the work and bought two of each. I helped her carry them to her car, a white Audi SUV. I remember the car because it had lovely lines, and I had always wanted to drive in one. I made an admiring comment about it and she said, *why, next time I come to visit you, we can go for a little drive.*

I was pleased, not so much with the offer but with the thought that she intended on becoming involved with the school. We were always recruiting parents for our school community council, and I hoped that she might consider becoming a member.

A couple of days later, I was doing lunch supervision when Sidney, a girl in grade nine, approached me.

You met my mom on Tuesday, she said by way of an opening.

I did?

Julie D. She's my mom. She bought some of those wooden things the school is selling.

Oh, yes. I remember. She seemed very nice. I didn't know she was your mother.

Uh huh. She said I should come tell you that she might like to buy some more soon, for her friends.

Well, that would be nice. Thank you, Sidney. I'd be happy to see her again.

She said you were a good person.

She did?

Yah. And she told me if I was ever upset about anything, it would be okay to come and tell you about it.

Well, that's part of my job, Sidney.

Okay. See ya'.

It was a funny little interaction but not entirely strange in context. Adolescents are often awkward socially. I thought it was sweet that Sidney had made an effort to connect with me, and I smiled as she bounced off to rejoin her friends. High schools are busy places, and I thought no more about the interaction. Several days later, Julie D. called me, sounding as though she had a really bad cold.

Would it be alright if I came in to buy another shelf?

Yes, of course. Happy to see you.

Is there a time that would be best?

No. I'm here all day. Anytime works. I try to leave around 5:30.

I'll come at 1:00. If you were available then, I would appreciate it.

Her tone sounded a bit off. Anyone could sell her a shelf. She didn't need an appointment for that, something I was sure that she knew. Once the students were back in class, I unpacked my own lunch and prepared to catch up on some emails. Julie Dillon strode into my office at 1:00 p.m. sharp and greeted me before seating herself.

Good. You're here. I need to talk with you. In private, if I may?

She gestured to the door. I took the hint and closed it. I sat back down and scrutinized her appearance. Expensive track suit today, stilettos, designer handbag, ponytail, and again with the oversized sun glasses. No pearls or rings this time but a rather substantial gold necklace with a thick chain circling her throat. I smiled at her expectantly, waiting for her to speak.

Do you have many shelves left?

We do. I gestured at the pile behind me on the cadenza.

I'll take two today. My friends really love them.

Uh. Great. Do you want to choose?

No. Anything will be fine.

I pushed my chair back, preparing to stand.

There's just this one thing I thought I should mention.

Yes?

It's about Sidney.

Yes?

She's a very sensitive girl, you know. Good natured and caring.

Yes. She seems great. Is everything alright here at school?

Oh, yes. School is fine. She's doing well.

Are you happy with her friend group?

Yes, yes. Lovely girls. She's known them since forever. They go to equestrian camp together. A couple of the girls, Jessie and Cass, have cottages on the same lake as ours. The girls are close. There's nothing to worry about there.

Can I help with anything?

Well, yes, maybe. If it comes up. Sidney is very sensitive, and bright, as I think you already know, and I worry that she is a little too sensitive at times. She gets herself worked up and then has trouble sleeping, you know. She's just started having these awful nightmares. And she wakes up with terrible headaches some days. I just thought you could keep an eye on her for me, here at school. In case she needed anything, for instance. I would want her to come to you personally. To know that she could trust you.

Yes, of course. Anything. I'm happy to help.

Well good. That's good then. Thank you. I really should go. Busy day.

Did you want those shelves?

Oh, yes. Yes, of course. Load me up!

Julie left with two pine shelves wedged between the handles of an oversized Louis Vuitton. It looked a bit odd. Actually, the whole visit had been a bit odd. I finished my lunch and busied myself with my unending pile of attendance reports. A week or so later, Sidney came to the front counter and asked the staff if she could book an appointment to see me.

They sent her to my office, and, without ceremony, she flopped in a chair and looked at me expectantly.

Can I help you?

You're good at helping people, right?

I try to be.

I know someone who needs help.

I see. Does she go here? Is it a student in our school?

No! It's about a friend of mine from someplace else.

I see. How can I help?

Her parents are always fighting and yelling and stuff. They smash things in the house, and the mom gets hit a lot.

That's not great.

No. And my friend doesn't like it. She doesn't ever get hurt or anything. but she gets scared.

I studied her while she was speaking. She was wearing expensive high-fashion clothing. Everything looked brand new and on trend. She had a stylish haircut, clear braces, and a delicate spray of freckles. But her hands were the giveaway. Fingernails chewed down to the small moons. Even as I watched, she was tearing at a cuticle, shredding the skin into a long peel half-way down the length of her finger. Tiny dots of blood rising to the surface were slowly appearing.

It sounds scary. How old is your friend?

She's my age. Fourteen.

Well, fourteen-year-olds need a safe and secure space to grow up in. If she doesn't feel safe there, we should let Children's Aid know about it.

Will they ask for her name?

Yes. And her address. And the school she attends. They need to make sure she's safe and that there is some support in place for the family.

Okay. I guess I better think about it. Sidney stood up.

Sidney, wait. Do I know this friend of yours?

No! She doesn't go here.

Okay. Well, if you think I might be helpful, will you promise to come back again to see me?

She beamed a brilliant smile at me before leaving.

I promise!

I was pretty sure by now that the friend was Sidney herself but that she didn't trust me well enough to unburden herself. I put in a call to

Children's Aid to see if there was an open file on the family. There was not. I spoke to an intake worker who told me that I didn't have enough to warrant an investigation. I was advised to keep a close watch on the girl and to get back in touch if anything changed.

Her mother, Julie Dillon, reappeared in my office the next morning. She was wearing the same track suit. The zipper done up all the way to her chin. As always, she looked immaculately groomed. I shut my office door.

Here for more shelves? I asked pointedly.

She looked startled by the abruptness of my question.

Julie, I am uncomfortable speaking with someone when I can't see their eyes. Would you mind removing your sunglasses when you're in my office? I'd really like to see your face.

I'm light sensitive, actually. I find them necessary.

Sidney came to see me yesterday. She was concerned about a friend of hers. A fourteen-year-old girl who she says doesn't attend here. Apparently, her parents fight all the time and smash things, and Sidney's friend is frightened.

You know, don't you?

She reached up and pulled off her sunglasses, setting them down on my desk. I read the brand name: BVLGARI. I looked at Julie. Two blackened eyes. Yellowish and purple bruising. Small cuts on her eyelids and eyebrows. He must have worn a ring when he hit her. I noticed the thick foundation she was wearing, carefully smoothed down her neck. She watched me studying her. Without saying anything, she undid the zipper on her jacket and opened the front slightly. Matching colours on the base of her throat. The bruises continued down her chest and likely beyond. I shuddered.

Have you called the police?

I can't.

Why not?

He's my husband.

So what? No one has the right to do that.

You don't understand.

Explain it to me.

He's a criminal lawyer. He knows people in the police department. Nobody would believe me.

Of course they would. Anyone looking at those bruises would believe you.

It's more complicated than you can imagine.

It looks pretty straightforward to me.

It only happens when he drinks. When he's working a big case. The pressure is awful for him, and he needs an outlet.

Most people go to the gym for that.

And he's a good father. We have a beautiful home and a luxurious lifestyle. I can't take that away from Sidney.

What do you mean?

Let's say I did have him charged. It would destroy his professional reputation. He'd lose clients, and then our income would suffer. I can't do that to Sidney. She's used to expensive things: nice vacations, the cottage, her own horse, pretty clothes, ballet, piano lessons.

You don't think that feeling safe in her own home is more important than that? Do you want her growing up believing that it's okay for men to assault women, or that it's okay for a man to abuse her?

Of course I don't want her to be afraid. Don't you see? That's why I'm here. I'm worried about her. She's not sleeping well. She's become clingy. She doesn't like to leave me alone with her father at night, even when she should be going to bed. I know that it's affecting her.

Then you need to do something. You're the grownup, and it's up to you to protect her.

I don't know how...

She broke down and began to sob. All sense of composure and pretense completely disappeared. I let her cry herself out. I needed the time to think. When she stopped weeping, I passed her a box of tissues and the compact mirror I kept in my purse. She accepted them wordlessly and began to dab at her face and eye makeup while I went to get her a glass of water. When I returned to my office, she was once again sitting upright, poised and calm, sunglasses in place.

You have options, I began. *If you don't want to call the police, you can just take Sidney and leave.*

He'd never let me go. Appearances matter to him.

The appearance of his wife with two shiners doesn't seem to bother him.

That's different. It's private. People don't know. We're both very careful.

Sidney knows, Julie. And she's worried about you. And it sounds like she may even be frightened of her own father. People will find out. Don't ask her to keep this kind of secret.

I knew I'd struck a nerve of sorts with that comment. Julie put her head in her hands.

I don't see a way out.

There are people we can call. We have a board social worker. She could help us. And there's a women's shelter nearby. I have their number. They have counsellors there who could help us. I know there are options.

Okay.

Okay?

Yes. Can you call Sidney out of class? I want her here. We can decide together.

Are you certain?

Yes.

A few minutes later, Sidney knocked on the door. When she saw her mother in my office, she ran across the room and threw her arms around her.

Mom! Are you okay? What happened? Did he hurt you?

The fear and panic in those words were heartbreaking. Julie pulled her daughter down onto the chair beside her. They hugged for a couple of minutes. I interrupted them.

Sidney, your mother has something important she wants to discuss with you.

They broke apart. Sidney looked at her mother.

Julie spoke first.

Sidney, you know that your daddy loves both of us very much. He's a good man and a good lawyer, and he would do anything for you.

Sidney's lip was trembling while she listened.

But the thing is honey, daddy's job is very stressful, and sometimes he doesn't handle that very well. You know what I mean, don't you, pookie?

Sidney nodded.

So, your principal and I have been talking, and she thinks maybe we should take a little vacation and live somewhere else for a little while. Until daddy feels better. What would you think about that, Sid?

That would be alright. I guess... if you want.

I think so, darling. Just until daddy and I sort some things out. Do you trust me?

Sidney nodded and her mother clasped her hands.

Okay. Good. Then we have a plan. We're not going to tell anyone about this Sidney; it's going to be our little secret for a few days. I need to set things up first. Can you keep this secret?

I'm good at secrets. I never told the other secret.

That's a good girl. I know you didn't, pookie.

Julie looked at me.

Call the shelter now. I'll speak to them.

I left Julie and Sidney in my office while Julie spoke to someone at the shelter. She was on the telephone for a long time. I paced in the hallways while I waited. I tried to picture the kind of man that could do that to someone he loved. Such violence was unfathomable to me. I thought of my own partner's hands: gently cradling our son, tenderly lifting his mother in and out of her wheelchair, caressing me. Thousands of images and all of them careful and kind and loving. I felt so unequipped to be helpful.

The office paged me to return when they were done. Both of them had been crying. The resemblance between the two had never seemed stronger. My heart broke to see such sadness.

It's not going to happen right away. I need a couple of days to get some cash and open a bank account somewhere new. And get clothes for both of us. I can stash some in the trunk of my car and some at the gym and maybe some in Sidney's locker.

They would make their escape before the weekend.

I didn't expect to hear from them for several days. I marked Sidney "absent with consent" for the rest of the week. And I fretted. The husband sounded volatile. I was worried about what might happen if he noticed the missing funds or found the packed clothing. I worried about Sidney, the secrets she was carrying and the pressure she was under. It was Wednesday or Thursday of the following week before I heard from Julie. She assured me that they were both safe and that nothing unexpected had happened. She had left her husband a goodbye note taped to a bottle of Scotch. The messaging had pleased her, and she was proud of her small feat.

I asked about her plans. Would she look for work? When would Sidney return to school? Were they getting counselling?

The shelter is awful, moaned Julie. *We sleep in a dormitory. The meals are all slop. I'm thinking that we should probably move to a hotel. We'd be more comfortable.*

How would you pay for it? Hotels need credit card deposits. Your husband would be able to locate you.

Well, he wouldn't mind, you know. I think he's already learned his lesson. I called him at his office this morning. He said we could come home, no questions asked.

You did what?!

Well, I thought he would be worried about Sid. I didn't want him worrying about her.

Julie, are you hearing yourself? What about you? Who's worrying about you?

I should go now dear; thank you for everything. I'm sure we'll find a way to sort it.

Julie, please, please don't do anything rash. Stay for some of the counselling sessions. Speak to the social workers. Don't put yourself in harm's way again. Please, for Sidney's sake.

She hung the phone up on me.

I didn't hear anything more about either Sidney or Julie Dillon. for a couple of weeks. Then the head of guidance came to see me with a request for Sidney's student records. She had apparently been registered as a boarding student in a nearby private girls' school. I took the request form to my office and slammed it down on a counter. Recklessly, I looked up Julie's home phone number and dialled it. She picked up on the first ring.

Hello, dear, I saw that it was you.

Julie, where are you and what are you doing?

Why, home of course. Things are all sorted. Tom has promised that it won't ever happen again. And the darling gave me diamond earrings as a welcome home gift. Everything's been lovely.

And Sidney?

Tucked up in a very nice girls' school. Very exclusive. She's safe and sound. It was Tom's idea. She can come home on weekends and holidays.

Julie, are you certain this is the right course? I'm worried about Sidney.

I heard the change in her tone immediately.

Listen, this is the truth: I don't want to be poor. I don't want Sid to be poor. Tom controls the money. So, Tom controls us. I would rather risk being here with him than living in a disgusting dormitory with no money.

I had no response for her. I had to swallow my judgment and bitter disappointment. Sadly, I knew that her daughter would learn that some relationships come with a price.

A Carton of Cigarettes

Warning: Scenes of sexual violence.

As a staff, we referred to Shawn and Shannon as the "double Ss." They were grade nine twins just starting high school. Shawn wore his dirty blonde hair shaggy and unkempt; Shannon wore hers clean and trim. He walked with a swagger, thumbs in his denim pockets. She cowered timidly in corners. He horked in the hallways, while she was careful not to leave a trace of herself anywhere. Despite their many differences, their facial features were almost identical. Uncannily so. Suspecting that each of them might welcome some independence, I made sure that they had different timetables and didn't share classes.

Shawn quickly established himself as a risktaker. Shannon was meek, eager to please, and deferential. Neither was strong academically. Shannon worked hard just to stay afloat, spending much of her time in our resource room. Shawn skipped classes, swore at staff, and made it clear that he didn't give a damn about school. On those rare occasions when he did attend, he often swore at a teacher, threatened a student, or started a physical altercation with someone. He didn't seem to need much provocation before he threw a punch or pulled out a knife.

It didn't take long for the staff to form strong opinions about Shawn. I had to deal with a constant stream of complaints about his behaviour. *You have to do something!* was a constant demand. There was little I could actually do, besides attempt to hold him accountable for the latest infraction and make the inevitable phone call home. Shawn's mother was parenting the twins alone and often worked double shifts at a local factory. Shawn's father had disappeared many years before. There were rumours that he was in prison for violent crime. Shawn's mother was exasperated by her son but felt powerless to control him. She frequently complained to me that he was running the streets at all hours and no longer listened to her.

It gradually became clear that Shawn had become part of a group of older teenagers involved in drug running. One day, he appeared at school with an eye swollen shut; his face badly beaten, and the sleeve of his jacket sliced through with multiple cuts. He had open wounds on his arms. Despite his tough-guy demeanour, he allowed me to administer some first aid and to sterilize and bandage the worst of his injuries. A couple of cuts were quite deep slashes and needed stitches. I asked a staff member to drive him to the hospital. When they returned to the school, I had a police liaison officer waiting to speak with him. Shawn wouldn't divulge anything and resumed his cocky manner.

In desperation, I called Shannon to my office and probed her gently. She disclosed that life at home was tension filled and unpleasant. Both she and her mother had become afraid of Shawn's outbursts of temper. According to Shannon, he ordered them around, came and went when he felt like it, hit Shannon, shoved his mother, and regularly frightened them. He also took their money and stole anything he could trade or pawn.

There's nothing we can do, Miss, she explained. *Shawn always does what he wants.*

Unwilling to write him off so early in his school career, I asked the youth officer to become involved. He arrived at the school one warmish fall day, perspiring heavily. Wearing his bulletproof vest and a belt stocked with baton, flashlight, walkie-talkie, and other equipment, he was also holstering a visible sidearm. A burly man, he looked particularly intimidating with all of his gear. Shawn was summoned, and despite all the officer's accoutrements, he was unimpressed. When he walked into my office, he looked at the officer and began to oink loudly.

The meeting did not produce the intended result. Afterwards, the officer told me that Shawn was running with a rough crowd and had already been initiated into a particularly nasty street gang. Small stuff mostly but dangerous nonetheless.

He looked at me and said, *It's only a matter of time until he gets picked up and thrown in jail. That may be the only thing that will shake him up.*

Changing my focus to Shannon, I told the staff that things at home were tough for her and anything we could do to help should be done.

We tried in small ways to compensate for her brother's behaviour.

Within months, Shawn had all but disappeared from school. I sent letters, notified the attendance counsellor, and reported him to Children's Aid, but nobody had any solutions. To be honest, he had become such an unpleasant presence that we were all secretly relieved not to have to deal with him. At the same time, we became aware that Shannon was blossoming with Shawn out of the way. I saw her socializing with friends, talking, and laughing. She began to wear lip gloss and eye makeup. She started accessorizing her outfits. She was less apologetic about her schoolwork and generally more confident. Many of us commented on the transformation.

Then, something changed for Shannon in second semester. A darkness seemed to have come over her. She stopped handing in her assignments and took to wearing loose-fitting, sloppy clothing. She stopped caring for herself in any visible way. She was sullen with staff members and neglectful of her friends. I called her mother to discuss the worrying signs. Mrs. Sappier had also noticed the abrupt change but was without an explanation. Her long hours at work meant that she was rarely home to spend time with her daughter.

We had a rotation of community health workers in the school one day a week. Shannon approached me one day and asked, *the doctors and nurses, Miss, do they do pregnancy tests?*

Things suddenly made sense. I took her to the health team and left her there for whatever tests or counselling they might offer. She would not be the first grade nine girl to go too far without taking precautions. I saw her a couple of days later and delicately asked if things had turned out alright.

No, Miss. They're not good.

Can I help, Shannon? Do you want to speak with someone in guidance?

No, Miss. You. Do you have time?

As soon as we arrived in my office, she began to cry. Deep gut-wrenching sobs. She was bent over in her chair, holding herself, and rocking forwards and backwards. I assumed she was pregnant and waited for her to calm herself. I sat beside her quietly and rubbed her back. Finally, she spoke to me. Soft broken whispery fragments only.

It was... only Shawn... at first...

What do you mean, Shannon?

When I... got out... of the shower...

I don't understand.

He pushed me... and climbed on me.... I... didn't know... why... or what... he was...

The truth of the situation was suddenly clear. My eyes stung with tears.

Does your mom know?

No.

Would you like me to call her?

She... can't...

Okay, try to relax now. You don't have to say anything else. I'll get some help.

His friends... they... watched and... took... turns...

I had to bite my bottom lip.

She was ashamed and frightened and still wanted to protect her brother while sparing her mother the truth. With her reluctant permission, I called the police and our social worker. Soon a small team of professionals was gathered at the school putting together a plan. Shannon was stoic. She answered their questions and provided details that I wanted desperately not to hear. She insisted that I stay with her, and she held my hand so tightly that my fingers went numb.

Although she was not pregnant, she had been gang raped on multiple occasions. Her brother let his friends in while she was sleeping or showering. She had ceased to struggle or attempt to defend herself because they seemingly liked the fight and used it as an excuse to hit her, as well as violating her in other ways. She told us that once, she was forced to stay still while two men raped her simultaneously, and a third pissed on her. She had learned to lie passively with her eyes closed. At first, she said, she had cried and begged her brother to make it stop, but he had done nothing to protect her. The police informed us that he had shown no remorse when he was arrested. He actually boasted that it was an easy way to get a carton of cigarettes.

I was told by the clinicians that it would be impossible for Shannon to fully recover from her trauma. To have such a thing done to her by a twin was among the most intimate of betrayals. They also expressed deep concern for Shawn and for what the assaults against his twin indicated about his state of mind. Between social services, victim services, and our connections with a mental health facility, we were able to quickly get Shannon and her mother new housing and counselling, as well as connecting them with support services. Shawn disappeared into the streets and never made it to his court appearance.

Almost a year later, I read in a local newspaper that Shawn had been killed in a knifing outside a bar. My first reaction was, "Thank God, now there's a real chance for Shannon to heal. She won't ever have to testify against him." I shocked myself with the thought. My job was to ensure the safety and wellbeing of all of my students. I had no right to think such a horrible thing. So I closed my eyes and willed myself to remember the look of him—a frightened fourteen-year-old boy, sitting in my office with his arm badly cut, deep knife slashes requiring stitches and that single moment of vulnerability when he allowed me to administer first aid.

Myah

I saw news of the fire in the paper. It was in a boarded-up house west of the school, close to a lake. Teenagers squatted there. There was no clear egress within the rabbit warren of small-connected rooms, and the rescue workers couldn't find their way through to all of the small cubbyholes. There were eight fatalities. All of them were young people. No names were released.

I was certain that one of our students was a victim. We hadn't seen her since shortly before the fire, and it was out of character for her to stay away for so long. I broke out in chills while reading the short news article. Something deep in my gut told me that Myah was among them. I sat there for the longest time trying to process my feelings. I was overcome with a deep sense of sadness and loss—the waste of a life filled with such joy and promise.

When I first met Myah, she was a round-faced girl with crazy blond braids and a vibrant collection of retro tops. She loved the Beatles and everything sixties, had embroidered large flowers on her jeans, and inserted triangular patches in the legs to create faux bell-bottoms. Her smile was infectious. I never learned why she left home. She was very private about her family history. She assured me and other staff members who expressed caring for her that she was fine. She claimed to have money and said she was well looked after. *Peace out* was one of the many throwback expressions she regularly used in conversation.

Myah was a good student. She was one of the girls that we hoped we could get into college or university. Our school was situated in an economically depressed part of the region, and many of our graduates went straight into the workforce. Myah was different. She showed up with her army surplus bag stuffed with organized binders and assignments and books. She high-fived everyone in the hall when she aced a test or a project. Her enthusiasm for her assignments was endearing. I loved to see her capering down the hall with her distinctively frayed bell-bottoms and cheerful countenance.

When Myah disappeared from the building for an extended period, we became alarmed. None of her friends knew where she was, or if they did, they weren't telling. All of the contact information we had for her was out of date. Weeks went by with no word. Finally, one day, I saw a girl in the smoking area that looked vaguely familiar. Her hair was cut short, hacked erratically with scissors, and her face was drawn and thin. Clothes hung loosely on her frame. I approached and the surrounding girls stepped back, allowing me private access.

Myah?

She looked up at me and held my gaze.

Myah, what happened to you? We've been so worried.

She nodded in acknowledgment, but her sunny smile and flower-power, give-peace-a-chance verve were gone. I was stunned by the change in her.

Come with me, I said, putting my arm around her shoulder. *We need to talk. I'm worried about you. Have you eaten today?*

She followed me to the office but was docile and without her usual bounce. I gave her some yogurt and fruit which she ate hungrily. I noticed that she was without her book bag.

Myah, you look dreadful. Have you been ill?

She shook her head.

Please tell me. Let me help you.

I can look out for myself. I don't need help.

Myah, please. What happened to you?

She sighed deeply.

Do you really want to know?

I nodded.

You promise not to call the cops?

Maybe.

No. You have to promise.

I can't promise that, Myah. I don't know what happened. Are you in trouble with the police?

No!

She shook her head.

Okay. I'll tell you, but you can't freak out on me. I'm fine.

I nodded.

You know I've been staying in this shelter. I left home, but my parents gave me money. They told me not to come back. That's all I'm going to say about that. So, I was staying in this shelter and going to school and working part-time at this twenty-four-hour convenience store, and everything was cool, right? I was getting good grades and stuff and going to graduate this year.

I smiled and nodded encouragingly.

But one night, I woke up 'cause someone was holding my hair tight and pulling it while they were grabbing and shoving at me, and they dragged me to the shower and then I got raped. It was pitch black, and I screamed but nobody came until after. I heard that you're not supposed to fight back, and that rape is about power, and so I didn't fight much. I just screamed.

I was horrified but resisted the urge to embrace her. Tears spilled from my eyes. I sat motionless, waiting for her to continue.

So after, I took my shit and found a place nearby. I'm squatting with some other kids. There's no water or heat or anything, but it feels safe. We have a propane camp stove and candles and bottles of water. It's better than the car I was sleeping in. I just need to finish my year, and then I'll have my diploma.

Myah, let me help you. Let me find you a better living situation. Maybe you can board with one of our families, or go home to your parents? Or we could apply for student assistance, and you could get your own place. I can arrange for counselling and a doctor's appointment. You need to be checked.

She shook her head as soon as I began to offer my suggestions.

I just need to finish my diploma and then everything will be fine.

I loaded her up with more yogurt, fruit, and some granola bars before she left my office. She stuffed these things into a used plastic bag I found in my drawer and smiled at me weakly before leaving. I resolved to myself that I would find some way of helping her. I called a contact at social services to see how long it would take to expedite some assistance. The worker there promised to help and suggested she could get an approval and cut a cheque in two weeks once the paperwork was done. I set a tentative meeting for her to meet Myah.

Later that day, I wanted to speak to Myah about the social assistance offer and went looking for her. I couldn't find her, and her friends claimed

not to know where she had gone. I continued to look for her over the next several days but then remembered that when she had shown up at school, she did not have her book bag. Worried, I contacted our police liaison officer and asked him if he knew where kids might be squatting. He had several suggestions but said that they were too dangerous for me to visit without an escort. He refused to tell me the exact locations but offered to look for her himself. I gave him a copy of her photo.

Several days later the officer dropped into my office and shook his head.

That shelter you mentioned. There've been lots of complaints. They're about to lose funding. They'll have to close.

And Myah?

No real luck, I'm afraid. There's a boarded-up house west of here, towards the lake. It's full of teenage squatters. I'm pretty sure she's there, but the kids won't say.

I nodded. The code of the street again. I had encountered this over and over again during my tenure and had not once ever found a way to pierce the embargo on information sharing. Although Myah did not return to school again, her marks were high enough to justify final credits being awarded even without her final exams and assignments. At commencement that year, an evening of unbridled celebration, I called her name aloud and waited a beat. A small possibility briefly flickered, and I held my breath a moment, hoping that she would suddenly appear and breeze across the stage with her distinctive swing.

Alyssa

A lyssa registered for school mid-October, just as we were preparing early progress reports. She showed up without an adult, carrying a previous year's report card, proof of address, and a sheaf of lined paper and some pens. She was ready for school. I scrutinized the report car—high fifties to low sixties. Not an academic student. Poor attendance record. She had arrived at school by sneaking onto one of the yellow buses in the morning and had no way of returning home except by the same way. She must have sidled up to a group of students and slipped on unnoticed.

I tried to call her mother to explain that she needed to be present to register her daughter. Her cell phone was turned off.

She works nights, explained Alyssa apologetically. *I'll take these home and bring them back tomorrow.*

She was a petite fourteen-year-old with neatly brushed shiny blonde hair, a sweet face with delicate features, and the tiniest bit of eyeliner. She wore warm boots, tights, an impossibly short kilt, likely from a previous school uniform, and a wrinkled white shirt. No winter coat. Her school supplies were in a plastic grocery bag. I couldn't register her without the signed forms. Neither could I send her home on foot without a winter coat. Getting her back on the bus at the end of the day would be interesting. I'd have to speak to the driver in person and explain that she was a new student. With luck, he'd agree to take her. Otherwise, I would have to drive her home.

I took her to student services, and we built her a timetable. The counsellor gave her a cafeteria coupon for lunch and walked her to class. What struck us both was how determined she was to get started. She wanted to be here. That was a good sign. She'll fit in easily.

The next morning, the office manager handed me a crumpled set of forms. The signature was suspiciously loopy with big flourishes and a happy face. It looked very much like the writing of an adolescent girl and not the scrawl of a shift-working single mom. I took the forms and went to my office, determined to reach Alyssa's mother. I called her cell phone repeatedly. I left multiple phone messages insisting that she call me back. I indicated that forged signatures might necessitate my calling the police and that I needed to ensure that Alyssa was living with a responsible parent.

Mid-afternoon I received a call back.

This is Sheri Torres. You called me.

I did. Thank you for calling back. Alyssa brought some forms in today, and I need to confirm that you signed them and that it was your intention to register her at our school.

Ya'. I work nights. She left me some stuff. I told her to go ahead and sign it for me. I had to get some sleep. The baby was screaming, and I didn't have time to read it all.

Thank you for clearing that up. I'll put a note on the paperwork that you have confirmed your intention to register her and that you gave her permission to sign the forms.

Ya'. Whatever. Look I'm bagged. I need to hit the shitter and feed the kid before I leave for work. You need anything else?

No. Just to say that Alyssa seems lovely. We're very happy to have her.

Ya'. Well don't be fooled. The girl's a little cunt. Lies all the time. Gets people to feel sorry for her. She makes trouble everywhere we go. You better watch her.

It's not every day you hear a parent call their own daughter a cunt. It's not so much that I was shocked as it was that I couldn't credit it. Alyssa's presentation had been polite and sweet and natural. It was hard to believe her mother's claims. I would watch her but not for signs of maliciousness so much as for signs of neglect.

For the rest of October and into November, I checked in with Alyssa once a week. She liked her teachers. She liked her courses. She was making friends. She looked clean and well groomed. She was open and chatty. There was nothing that set off alarm bells. I passed her cafeteria coupons to ensure she ate a good lunch. She frequented the breakfast club so I knew she had something to eat each morning. Her teachers liked her and said she was managing her schoolwork. I thought things were on track.

And then one Friday afternoon, she showed up at my office door and asked if she could come in for a minute to talk to me.

Of course, sweetie. Have a seat. What's going on?

I have to see my grandparents this weekend.

So, that's a nice thing, isn't it?

Not really. They're mean to me.

What do you mean?

They're my mom's parents. They live in the country on this scary road in the middle of nowhere. And they're always yelling at me. They say horrible things.

Like what?

Like I'm a piece of garbage. And I'm worthless and stupid and lazy.

Why would they say those things to you?

They hate me. I'm the reason my mom's life is fucked up.

Why would they think that?

Because she got pregnant with me when she was fourteen and was afraid to tell them until it was too late for an abortion. They didn't want me. She didn't neither.

I'm sure they want you now, Alyssa. You're smart and lovely and kind.

No. They like my little sister, Ellie, and they're good to her, but they hate me.

Are you sure you're not exaggerating?

She shook her head.

I'm not, you know.

Large tears were slowly falling down her troubled face. She dabbed at her eyes with the sleeve of her blouse, and a smear of blue eyeliner left a long smudge on the fabric. We both looked at the stain.

What would you like me to do?

There's nothing.

Shall I try to phone your mother?

She's sleeping.

Can I ask her to leave you at home?

No! She's planning a party with her friends this weekend and wants to get rid of me and Ellie.

Is there somewhere else you could go? A friend's house, maybe?

She won't let me. They need me to look after Ellie.

Is there anything else, Alyssa? Have you told me everything?

I should go.

It's my job to make sure you're going to be safe when you leave here. It doesn't sound like you feel safe with your grandparents.

I don't. But I have to look after Ellie.

Let me call your mom.

Slowly, she looked up at me through teary eyes. A wet despondent face. She nodded. I picked up the phone and called her mother.

Hi, Ms. Torres, I'm calling from the high school. I'm sorry to bother you, but I have your daughter in the office, and she's a little upset. I thought that you would want to know.

What's the little bitch got up to?

Alyssa told me that she's not looking forward to seeing her grandparents this weekend. She told me that they often abuse her verbally and...

You stop right there and mind your own fuckin' business. My parents put up with all kinds of shit from her. I need a goddamn break. They're coming to take her and Ellie for the weekend so I can have some kind of a life. She's a fuckin' selfish little bitch.

She's only fourteen, Ms. Torres. And I have a duty to report if I believe a child is being abused or neglected in any way.

Well, you just goddamn go ahead and call Children's Aid. They already got a file on her three-feet thick. She always pulls this kind of shit.

I would have said more, but she hung up the phone. I looked at Alyssa who was now curled up in a little ball on the chair, crying softly. I called Children's Aid and asked for her worker. They were able to connect me fairly quickly, and I outlined the events, and then they asked to speak with Alyssa. I passed Alyssa the phone and she told her worker exactly what she had told me. She ended the call by saying, *Yes, I will.*

How did that go?

She said I have to go.

Really?

Yes. But if they start on me again, I have to be polite and not yell back but just tell them I want to leave the room. And then I have to read a book or do some homework or something.

Are you alright with that?

Yes. I want to stay with Ellie.

She went back to class, and I called Children's Aid back. I spoke to her worker.

Look, she said, *I'm in the city. I can't get to her for at least two hours. School will be over by then. I'll come by next week and check on her. It's complicated. Her grandparents used to have custody, and there's history there.*

Why did they have custody?

Her mother was in jail. They had Alyssa for almost three years.

Were they good to her?

By all reports. She attended school. Got good marks. The only complaints came from her grandparents. They said she was mouthy. The worker went in to work with the three of them.

You weren't the worker then?

No. Different district. The file got passed to me when they moved here.

But you're in the city?

I commute.

It was a frustrating situation. There was nothing more that I could do. On Monday morning, I checked in with Alyssa. She was fairly quiet but assured me that everything had been fine. She told me that her grandparents had been okay and that all was well. I noted the dark shadows under her eyes. She looked as though she had slept badly, but I did not probe further.

Alyssa continued to attend regularly and was earning acceptable grades. All seemed to be going fairly well. And then, one Monday morning, she missed school, and no one called in her absence. The following day, I watched her get off the bus, shoulders slumped, head down, taking small shuffling steps. Mid-morning, between phone calls, I thought I should check in on her. She was guarded and said that she would talk to me later. At the beginning of lunch, she appeared at my office and asked for a cafeteria coupon. She followed me to my desk while I retrieved one.

You okay?

She nodded.

You sure?

She nodded again.

You look pretty upset.

Her lips began to tremble, her eyes filled with tears, and she nodded for a third time. I shut my office door, and we sat down together.

Can you tell me?

My mom and I got in a fight on the weekend.

Is that why you weren't here yesterday?

Yes.

What happened?

She came home from work on Friday and it was payday, and she was carrying this big bag, and I thought maybe it was groceries or toothpaste or shampoo because we were out of everything, but it was a big bag of booze. Beers and vodka and coolers and shit. And there was no bread in the house and nothing to feed Ellie, and I totally lost it, and I screamed at her.

I'm guessing that didn't go well.

No. She called me a bunch of names and went to her room and slammed the door.

And?

And then I went to take a hot shower to relax and calm down and...

And?

She pulled me out of the shower and dragged me to the front door and pushed me outside without any clothes on, just a towel and no shoes, and locked me out. She said if I didn't like the decisions she made, I could find somewhere else to live.

My God, Alyssa, in this weather? What did you do?

I ran to the neighbours. It wasn't that far. I pounded on the door until they woke up and they let me in and called the police.

Oh, honey, I'm so sorry. What happened?

The police came, and they went and talked to her, and she was all nice to them and stuff, and she told them that I was a liar, and I'd run away after she'd told me off for not babysitting Ellie proper. And that's such a rotten thing to make up. I love Ellie, and I always look after her.

Did they believe her?

They drove me to my grandparents' house.

Oh, God. Then what?

She had already phoned them to say I was coming, and they believed her. And they ragged on me and told me I got what I deserved.

Where are you staying now?

They brought me home last night. I told her she was the liar, and then my grandfather slapped me really hard.

Did anyone call Children's Aid?

I don't know.

We should tell your worker.

She nodded, and I made the call. I put Alyssa on the line and had her recount the story again for her worker. Afterwards, I sent her to the cafeteria to get some lunch. I was increasingly worried; she seemed to be telling the truth, and I was afraid that she was at risk. Other than speaking to her worker and begging for an intervention, which I had already done, there didn't seem to be anything else that I could do.

Weeks went by, and then Alyssa came to me just before the January exams. She looked wrung out. Her hair was unwashed, and she wore a slovenly t-shirt and ripped leggings.

I have to talk to you.

Of course. Come in.

Can I shut the door?

Of course.

I waited for her to take a seat and to compose herself. She sat stiffly in a chair, looking uncomfortable. She had balled up her winter coat and was clutching it like a pillow or a stuffy.

It's about what happened this weekend.

What happened?

My mom was out at a bar. She had the weekend off. I was babysitting Ellie. I heard her come in about three o'clock in the morning. I heard a car door slamming. She brought home some guy, and they went downstairs to the basement. I went back to sleep.

I waited quietly while she paused to order her thoughts.

And then I woke up. He had his hand down my pajamas, and he'd undone his pants, and he was in my bedroom and was telling me that I was beautiful and that I needed to be very quiet.

A wave of terror washed over me. My eyes filled with tears. I resisted the urge to move or to interrupt her. I waited for her to continue.

And I shoved him and yelled and yelled at him, and I yelled for my mom, and I ran out of my room, and I found her passed out in her bed, and I shook her and told her what he was doing in my room, and she just rolled over.

What did you do then, honey?

I picked up Ellie, and I ran to the neighbours.

Did they call the police?

Ya', they did. And everyone said how brave I was.

And what about your mom?

I stayed at the neighbours with Ellie and went home the next morning.

And she was just waking up. Really hungover. She told me I did the right thing.

That's good then, Alyssa. I'm glad she said that.

That was Saturday night.

Yes?

And then on Sunday, she invited the guy to come over and told me he was going to apologize.

No!

And he came and said he didn't know what he was doing. He said he was sleepwalking. And my mom said I had to tell the police I made it up so he wouldn't lose his job or go to jail.

What did you do?

I didn't know what to do so I just stood there.

Oh, honey, I'm so sorry. That should not have happened to you. You should not have had to see him again. None of it should have happened.

She looked at me solemnly. She was tired. Numb. I was horrified.

Was Ellie alright?

She nodded. *I don't think he touched her.*

Have you talked to your worker?

She called the house last night. She said I have to go and live with my grandparents.

What?!

My mom told the worker I was too much trouble and that she could do a better job of looking after Ellie if I wasn't always creating situations.

But your worker believed you, surely?

I think so. The police arrested the guy.

I walked her to a quiet space in our guidance area. She settled onto a couch with pillows and a fuzzy blanket. I knew that staff would check on her and hoped that she might get a little sleep. I went back to my office and called the school liaison officer who confirmed her story. Then I called Children's Aid and waited to speak with her worker. She told me the file was being transferred to another district and that she would no longer be the worker. She also told me that Alyssa's grandparents would register her in a new school by the end of the week. The school was out of our district and far away from the friends she had made here. It was an unbelievable sequence of events. She was only fourteen. It would be her third high school in one academic year. Any learning gains would be lost in the transition. She would once again be friendless and without a consistent advocate. I knew that she felt unsafe with her grandparents.

I called everyone I could think of. I consulted with the police, the school board lawyer, and our social worker. I called her grandparents and begged them to drive her to our school for the balance of the school year. I wrote a letter to Children Aid's challenging their handling of her case. Nothing made a difference. Her grandfather brought her to school to empty her locker and she came to say goodbye to me. I hugged her tightly, trying to squeeze in as much love as I could. *I'm just worried about Ellie* was the last thing she said to me.

Brooke and Lewis

The semester had started, and we were already a couple of months into term when I received a registration appointment for a new student. Mrs. Reed, the mother, appeared promptly at the designated time accompanied by our new student, a pleasant looking young boy she introduced as Lewis. I picked up the file, read the file label, and hesitated. The registration paperwork had been completed for a student named Brooke. I glanced up at Mrs. Reed and saw her eyeing me.

The paperwork says that you will be registering Brooke today, I began.

Yes, agreed the mother. *And this is Brooke.*

Oh, I'm sorry, I thought you introduced him as Lewis. My mistake. I apologize.

In truth, I was a little confused.

Brooke is fourteen and is undergoing gender reassignment. She would prefer to be known as Lewis.

Certainly, I tried to recover quickly. *In the interim, shall we build a timetable for Lewis?* I looked at Lewis encouragingly and asked them what their favourite subjects were.

I don't like school much. English, I guess, and art and gym and drama.

Well, I don't recommend putting all of those subjects together in one semester. We should balance things out and give you two academic subjects and two electives. That will ensure that you aren't overloaded with too much homework at one time. Does that sound okay?

Mrs. Reed responded.

Lewis will need a good math teacher. Someone who gives a lot of extra help. I don't want to have to pay for a math tutor. We have enough medical appointments without worrying about tutoring.

Would it be better if we saved math for second semester? I could give Lewis English and geography in the morning, followed by drama and gym in the afternoon.

Lewis whispered something to his mother.

Will Lewis use the boys' showers and change room for gym?

I paused.

I don't know, really. Is that the preference?

And which bathroom will he use? The male one?

I swallowed hard and sat back in my chair. *Which one would Lewis like to use?*

Really! said Mrs. Reed in an aggrieved tone. *This is such a backwards school! I would have thought that someone in your position would be better prepared to support my son.*

I was taken aback by her anger.

We're very happy to support Lewis, Mrs. Reed. I'm simply inquiring after their preference and yours regarding such things as bathrooms and changing rooms. I have no way of knowing what Lewis is comfortable with unless I ask.

Better schools than yours have gender-neutral accommodations. I'm surprised frankly, that you do not seem to have these things.

We do have wheelchair facilities—showers, change rooms, and bathrooms—and I can give Lewis a key to those areas in the interim.

I looked at Lewis.

Would that work for you, Lewis?

They nodded at me, and I smiled in return. We concluded our appointment and agreed that Lewis would start school on the following Monday. Before they left, I asked Lewis a simple question.

Do you have any friends here, Lewis?

Mrs. Reed froze and looked at me with daggers.

Lewis answered.

I know some kids from a couple of years ago in elementary school. But then I went to school in another board and became Lewis. They might know me as Brooke. I don't know if they'll remember me.

Maybe your parents can help you prepare a response if they recognize you and ask questions. You'll have time over the weekend to talk about it. It's helpful to practise such things.

Mrs. Reed swept out of my office without any pleasantries, and Lewis followed after her. I sat there for several minutes trying to think of ways I might have better responded. I picked up the phone and conferred with a colleague at the board. He assured me that the most important thing now was to ensure that strict confidentiality was maintained. The sharing of such private information was to be their decision. I arranged for gender-neutral/wheelchair signage for the designated bathrooms, shower, and changing room.

On the following Monday, I waited in the front foyer to greet the students as they arrived. I noted that Lewis arrived on a school bus and that they seemed to have already made a friend. They walked past me with a male student and headed towards their locker as though they were entirely comfortable. I was pleased to see them looking so relaxed.

On Friday afternoon, a group of grade nine girls asked to see me in my office. The little delegation piled in and took seats around the board-room table. I passed them a candy jar with chocolate caramels and waited to hear what they had to say.

It's about the new kid, began one of the girls. *We know that it's Brooke. We were in elementary school together.*

I groaned inwardly. I wasn't prepared to have other students confronting me about Lewis.

I'm not sure why you're telling me this, I responded. *If you have something to say about Lewis, I think you should say it to Lewis. I don't have anything I can say to you about this.*

Is it true? asked one of the others.

If this is what you want to speak with me about, I'm afraid you'll have to leave. I don't like gossip.

The small group stood and clustered at my doorway, a couple of them were pouting.

We just wanted to know.

Goodbye ladies. Nice to see you. Get to class!

I was worried about what might happen next. I knew enough to know that teenagers can be generous and compassionate, but they can just as easily turn and be cruel. Bullying issues are not uncommon in a high school, particularly in grades nine and ten.

The following week, Lewis appeared at my office door first thing in the morning. I invited them in, and they sat down in one of the guest chairs by my desk.

People know, they announced in a shrill shriek. *They know!*

I nodded.

What have you told the other students?

I said that Brooke was my twin sister.

Did they believe you?

Maybe. Some did.

Lewis was smiling at their clever subterfuge. They looked smug. My stomach started to churn. I had a feeling that this wouldn't end well.

Has there been any issue with the change room and showers?

No one said anything. But some of the guys are wondering about it.

What can I do to help?

Nothing. I just thought you should know. In case something happens.

Lewis added this last bit airily. I was concerned that Lewis did not fully appreciate the full extent of what was possible—an ugly backlash that might be unleashed.

Like what? What do you think will happen?

I don't know exactly. Maybe something bad. I'm not sure.

Lewis, this is your decision and your life. I want you to feel safe here. If something or someone gives you a bad feeling, I want you to tell me. Okay?

Lewis's safety and wellbeing was paramount, and I needed to reinforce this. I had a dreadful feeling that things might escalate. I wanted them to feel free to tell me what was happening.

They smiled at me.

Okay. Thanks!

Two weeks later, on Halloween, Lewis did something completely surprising: They showed up for school dressed as a Playboy bunny. Lewis wore a revealing and sexy outfit; cleavage and curves on full display, jewelry, styled hair, makeup, stilettos, bunny ears, and tail. They could easily have passed for a seventeen-year-old girl. By the end of the morning, the whole school was abuzz, and Lewis's secret was out in the open. The girls who had come to see me about Lewis earlier gave me the stink-eye when they passed. I assumed that after their initial shock, they would settle down. Soon, I hoped, someone else or some other issue would become the subject of interest.

I was surprised again, however, by a visit from Lewis the following morning. Dressed in girls' clothing, Lewis stood before me, looking every bit a teenage girl. Dangly earrings, push-up bra, and glittery makeup.

Lewis looked at me defiantly, challenging me to say something.

Good morning! I greeted them cheerily.

Do I look like Brooke today?

I have no idea. What does Brooke look like?

Like this!

They gestured with a flamboyant sweep of their arms.

Okay. Great. Then I guess so.

Wasn't yesterday fabulous! They enthused. *I really fooled everyone.*

Is that what you wanted?

I want to wear what I feel like. I enjoy being a girl sometimes.

Okay. Cool. As long as you're comfortable.

You aren't going to lecture me?

About what? You're free to dress however you want, Lewis.

Call me Brooke when I look like this.

You're not afraid of confusing your friends?

No. My friends really like it.

Well then, that's great. I'm glad you feel supported.

Brooke left my office and went to class. It wasn't clear to me what Lewis/Brooke was communicating. What was certain, however, was that there would be some sort of repercussion among the other students. I worried that the boys' gym class, in particular, might cause them some difficulty.

What I didn't realize at the time but learned later on, was that Lewis/Brooke's divorced parents were not equally supportive of the gender-reassignment process. While Mrs. Reed was strongly in favour of it, Mr. Reed felt that Lewis/Brooke was too young to make such an important decision. As a result, when Lewis/Brooke visited with their father, they dressed and acted as Brooke. When Lewis/Brooke returned home to their mother, they reverted to dressing and acting as Lewis.

Simmering under the surface at school was a worrying peer group issue. Lewis, like many grade nines, was sexually active and, as Lewis, had engaged in sexual activities with a couple of grade nine girls. Subsequent to Brooke's reappearance, those grade nine girls now felt betrayed and upset. What also came out was that Brooke had been sexually active in grade eight, as Brooke, and had engaged in activities with at least three boys who were now in grades nine and ten. Those boys were now being called *freaks* and other sexually derogative terms. As a result, they wanted to beat the crap out of Lewis and were threatening them.

When word of the threats reached Mrs. Reed, she phoned me and demanded that I put a stop to the bullying.

I should have known that you were not capable of handling Lewis's situation, was her parting shot.

At the same time, other parents were now complaining that a girl was taking a boy's gym and health class, and that their sons were uncomfortable.

Lewis, as Lewis, continued to flirt with the girls. This created further backlash from the boys who felt that Lewis did not have the right to do so and that Lewis was impinging on their territory. Several physical altercations ensued, but Lewis seemed to relish the attention they were receiving, even though they were often outnumbered and physically hurt.

One day when Brooke appeared at school, they again dropped by my office.

What do you think of my outfit?

I think you look very nice.

I saw my psychiatrist last night. I thought you would be interested.

Oh?

He said that I probably shouldn't go through with the gender reassignment right now.

Oh?

Yeah, he said he thinks that I'm really what they call gender-fluid. That I like going back and forth.

Okay.

So, I'm going to choose a new name. A name that will be my gender-fluid name. So, I can go back and forth and not confuse people.

That sounds like a great idea.

I want a good name. A name that describes me.

Well, that's important. You shouldn't rush into choosing. Why not go to the library and print off a list so you can think about it?

A week or so later, a large group of students rushed outside to watch a fight taking place in the parking lot. Staff called me, and we hurried outside to break things up. Lewis had initiated a fight with a senior student who had been taunting them. The older boy was much taller and heavier than Lewis and had quickly got the upper hand, subjecting Lewis to a terrible beating. I suspended both students. Lewis threw a tantrum in my office when I explained that they would be suspended.

They swore at me and told me that I was not supportive, that the entire school hated them, and that I had done nothing to be helpful. When I called home to inform Mrs. Reed, she took the same tone with me. She accused me of not understanding Lewis's needs and of running a *shit school*. Lewis was by now lying on the floor in my office, kicking their legs and screaming. When I knelt beside them in an attempt to calm them, they began to smash their head on the floor with such force that I feared serious injury. I pulled Lewis into my lap and held them there until they were soothed. When Mrs. Reed arrived to take Lewis home, I asked that Lewis not return to school until they had been seen by a doctor.

A couple of days later, I received a call from Mr. Reed. He informed me that Brooke was now residing with him and would be registered in a private girl's academy. I believe that the push-and-pull between the parents, the ordinary pressures and anxieties of being an adolescent, and the turmoil about their sexual identity and self-expression were so challenging that Brooke/Lewis had simply been overwhelmed by the weight of it all. I have no idea if the freedom of gender fluidity would eventually bring joy to their young life, but I hoped so.

Chanelle

Early in November, Chanelle vanished from school without explanation. She was a stunning grade eleven girl with a lovely smile who could have easily been taken for a model. Although she was shy by nature, her disposition was sweet, and she was well liked by everyone. The phone number listed for her was out of service, and the address she had provided for the family home turned out to be the local convenience store. This was not an unusual occurrence, as many of our families were transient and preferred not to disclose personal information. Staff asked Chanelle's friends about her whereabouts, but they claimed not to know where she was or what she was doing. A cloud of secrecy shrouded Chanelle, as other teens in the community attempted to provide her with a protective buffer. I suspected that she had dropped out of school for a short-term job somewhere. Often when there was an opportunity at the Diamond, a local biker bar, pretty girls would stop attending school and table dance for cash.

Chanelle had a brother who was registered as a student, but we almost never saw him. Tyrone was nineteen and should have graduated, but his attendance was so poor that he still had credits to earn. Word was that Tyrone had got involved with a local gang and that the income he earned from his various activities was supporting the family: his mother and two sisters. When Chanelle disappeared, I put the word out to some of the students that I would like to speak with Tyrone. I knew the neighbourhood network would deliver my message.

A couple of days later, Tyrone strolled into the building looking nonchalant and cool. He was tall, well over six-foot something, and dressed in baggy streetwear with multiple chains hanging down from his neck. A large cubic zirconium stud flashed from his right ear. I sidled towards him, not too close, and made eye contact, which he just barely acknowledged with an almost imperceptible nod before loudly sucking his teeth, followed by horking a large gob of phlegm on the terrazzo floor. I saw the onlookers elbow one another with admiration. He was making a point: You wanted me—and I came—but I do what I want. It was an elaborate ritual, and I waited for him to saunter more closely.

You want me?

I want to know how Chanelle is. Will she be returning to school?

What you asking for?

I haven't seen her in two weeks. I'm concerned about her.

She be coming back.

Tyrone turned abruptly and left the foyer through the front doors. I assumed he had a friend waiting to pick him up. But suddenly, his brief appearance turned into something critical. Not only had word reached Tyrone that I wanted to see him, but word had also reached rival gang members that he was intending to drop in. A confrontation with someone at the edge of the school property took place as soon as he went outside, and the commotion was audible from inside the building. Students who had seen the exchange from their classroom windows left their desks and ran outside to crowd around the combatants. I followed at speed, along with a number of staff members.

Tyrone was enraged. When I arrived, he was bashing a young man's head against the roadside curb, and blood was streaming from the victim's split skull. Staff members pulled Tyrone off the boy, and Tyrone ran away, the sleeves and front of his hoodie saturated with blood. I called for an ambulance and the police. With some difficulty, we were able to return the crowd of students back to class once the first responders appeared. The police took statements from some of the witnesses and began a search for Tyrone. Later, they informed me that the boy assaulted by Tyrone had suffered extensive and likely irreparable brain damage.

Chanelle returned to school a couple of days later. I intended to speak with her, but the school was still abuzz with excitement, and I found myself very busy. The police swung by regularly to conduct interviews. They were still unable to locate Tyrone and were scouring the neighbourhood for him. Chanelle continued to attend school but seemed deeply preoccupied. I had forgotten to ask about her unexplained absence.

Several days passed, and the police presence was still quite visible in the area. A liaison officer came into the school at least once a day to check in with Chanelle and ask her if she had heard from her brother. I was often present during these brief interviews and noticed that Chanelle was agitated by the repeated questioning. She shifted in her chair uncomfortably, twisted the corner of her shirt in a tight spiral, and didn't make eye contact. One morning, after Tyrone had been missing for more than five days, I noticed Chanelle taking food from the breakfast program into the library. Food in the library was forbidden, one of those iron-clad school rules that remains ubiquitous, and I followed her, intending to gently redirect her to the commons area.

To my astonishment, a tall, hoodie-clad figure rose from a darkened corner of the library to meet her. I couldn't see his face, but I knew by the size of him that it was her brother. I crossed the room quickly and stood between them, laying my hand gently on Tyrone's arm.

Let's sit.

I expected him to run, push past me, and make his escape. I was surprised when he sat down. Chanelle and I sat on either side of him. I could tell that he was tired. Tired enough to surrender.

How long have you been here?

The whole time.

It was my idea, offered Chanelle. *He couldn't come home.*

Why not?

My mama would have called the po-po.

Really?

For sure.

Did you spend the weekend in here?

He nodded.

You know it's my job to call the police.

Don't do it, Miss, pleaded Chanelle. *They'll hurt him.*

It will be better if he goes voluntarily, Chanelle. He can't hide forever. Why not cooperate and tell his side of the story?

I spoke into my walkie talkie.

Please call Officer Franks and tell him "I have what he wants in the library."

We heard the sirens within the minute. Chanelle began to cry but Tyrone comforted her in a low voice, shushing her. Even in the dim lighting, I could see crusty scabs on the side of his face and the back of his hands. These must have been from the last altercation. Chanelle and

Tyrone stayed seated at a table in the library with me. I patted Tyrone's arm lightly, attempting to keep him calm and reassured. He half stood a couple of times but sat down again, defeated. A group of armed officers burst into the library and pulled Tyrone to his feet. Chanelle screamed as they led him away in handcuffs. Our school liaison officer stayed behind to interview us.

As we crossed the hall to my office, I observed dozens of students watching glumly while Tyrone was placed in the police car. It dawned on me that they were his friends and must have known where he was. They had been complicit in hiding him in plain sight. The revelation shocked me, making me realize once again how powerful the code of the street was.

In my office, the interview with Chanelle began. The officer had specialized training and was gentle with her.

So, how long have you known where Tyrone was?

A few days.

But you knew we were looking for him?

Yes.

Did your mother know where he was hiding?

No.

Is there a reason why you didn't tell her?

She would have whooped his ass and turned him in...

So, you don't think she would have protected him?

Chanelle began to cry. She shook her head to indicate no.

Why is that, Chanelle?

She done with him.

Officer Franks looked surprised, but he continued with his probing.

Can you tell me why that is?

She continued to cry and held out her left hand. The fingers were slightly disfigured and misshapen. I hadn't noticed this before.

On account of him.

The officer and I were both puzzled. It looked as though her fingers had been broken and had not healed correctly. I assumed that Ty had accidentally hurt her somehow.

Chanelle, you have to explain. It might help Tyrone if we know exactly what has been happening.

She shook her head and sat there crying.

Would it help if the officer left the room? Would you tell me?

She nodded, and Officer Franks left the room somewhat reluctantly. I waited for several minutes while she composed herself.

I been awhile with no period, and my mama heard me be sick. She knew what was. She asked me, but I wasn't saying who. When I dint say, she tied me to a chair and bent my fingers and then I told.

What did you tell her, Chanelle?

Ty.

Ty what?

Ty sleep with me. Since we were little, he always did, but he didn't mean no harm by it.

Ty was the father of your baby?

She nodded.

And our mama said he best not come round no more.

I nodded to show I understood.

And the baby?

Mama made one of her brews.

I'm so sorry.

Sorry don't make no difference to nothing. My mama got her ways. Is Ty gonna be alright?

He's facing pretty serious charges, Chanelle. But the police will be fair.

I couldn't help but remember my own mother's excitement when I told her I was pregnant.

My baby having a baby! was her happy response. A smile so wide the contours of her face had changed. She had inundated us with gifts, a rocking chair, special towels, toys, and outfits. Her excitement was infectious; her interest in the minutiae of my pregnancy and her prospective grandchild was far gentler and more loving than she had been in many years. The prospect of my motherhood had softened her again, taken her back to a time when nurturing was prioritized. I struggled to understand Chanelle's protection of Tyrone. There were street codes I could only glimpse, just as there were astonishing examples of tight bonds within families.

Chloe

The front foyer of the school was filled with backpacks, hockey bags stuffed with gear, and sleeping bags. Sleepy fourteen-year-olds were trying to ignore their parents who were lingering, waiting to watch them board the bus for leadership camp. It was a familiar scene. As an experienced principal, I had learned to book an entire school bus simply for the excess luggage. It is a universal truth that grade nine girls will always pack everything they own when travelling anywhere overnight. Two nights at grade nine camp meant they brought clothes, bedding, snacks, and stuffies. And in no way were the boys more circumspect in their packing. They crammed every piece of sports equipment they owned into hockey bags, along with the usual overnight kit and sleeping bags. It didn't matter how specific we were about what to pack: teens had very different understandings about the meaning of the word "essential."

Before the bus pulled out of the parking lot, I climbed aboard for a few moments to intone my usual lecture.

School rules apply twenty-four-seven, no girls in the boys' cabin, no boys in the girls' cabin, no smoking, no drinking, no substance abuse. Your counsellors must be listened to at all times, any breach of these rules and your parents will be called to pick you up.

They had already signed behaviour contracts, as had their parents, but I thought it prudent to reiterate the rules before they left. A group of parents remained to wave when the departing buses finally pulled out.

I have learned that it's not possible to take over one hundred students away anywhere and not have something go wrong, despite the best contingency planning. What would it be this time? Broken limbs, sprained wrists, bee stings, and homesickness were typical. Occasionally, one of the youth counsellors might sneak in a package of cigarettes, but all of these things were manageable and easily dealt with. I knew that it was only a matter of time before I heard from staff with an update on the newest infractions.

Day one passed without significant incident. My vice-principal checked in with me at every meal time and at lights out. We took the extra precaution of hiring security to do the night patrols, and I was happy to hear that so far, all was well. Day two reports were also positive. Everyone was fitting in, the meals were fine, and there were no tears or first aid issues. Then a text came mid-morning on day three.

Call me. Issue in the cabins last night.

I grabbed my coat and headed outside the building to get the best cell phone reception.

Was anyone hurt? was my first question.

Not exactly. Not sure really. It's a bit confusing.

Start at the beginning so I can understand.

We heard rumours that started in the showers this morning. The girls in cabin three said they woke up to find Hunter in their cabin. He was apparently in Chloe's sleeping bag—with Chloe. They were both naked.

Oh my God. What did you do?

We pulled Chloe and Hunter from the breakfast room, and I interviewed them separately in the staff cabin.

What did Chloe say?

She said that Hunter kissed her in the woods yesterday and asked if he could visit her at night. He waited until the other girls were asleep and just came in and climbed into her sleeping bag.

Didn't the other girls wake?

No. Chloe said they just cuddled and fell asleep together.

With their clothes off?

Yup.

What did Hunter have to say for himself?

His story was a little different. He said they made out in the woods after the high-ropes course, and Chloe told him to come to the cabin at night. She left the door ajar when everyone was asleep. When he got there, she was standing starkers in the cabin waiting for him.

Why didn't he turn around and run?

Because he's a teenage boy, for Pete's sake! What do you think?! What teenage boy do you know that would run?!

But he's older than her. He's eighteen. She's fourteen. Her parents will have a fit.

Which is why I thought you would want to be the one who called them.

Yes, of course. Thanks.

The *thanks* was sarcastic. We both knew the call would be difficult.

How many staff cars are there? I'll call Chloe's parents and let you know if they're coming up to camp, or if I need you to have her driven back. Were the kids remorseful?

Not really. Hunter was sheepish. Chloe said she didn't know what the big deal was because they were in love and what they did was their business.

Oh God. Listen, great job. Did the security watch pick up on anything?

No. I checked. I did a bed check at midnight, and everyone was where they were supposed to be. It must have happened after midnight. The patrol didn't see anything.

My call with Chloe's father did not go well. I gave him few details, only enough to let him know that Chloe had visited with a boy in her cabin in the night. Her father immediately accused me of picking on his daughter and asked why, in a cabin full of girls, I had arbitrarily decided that Chloe was the one visiting with the boy. I invited him to come to the school and meet with me, Chloe, and the staff when they arrived back from camp.

You'll be hearing from my lawyer! he huffed before hanging up on me.

I texted my vice-principal and asked that Chloe be driven back to the school with a staff member.

I braced myself for what I assumed would be an ugly meeting. Holding kids accountable for their actions was a key part of my job, but doing so was always more difficult when parents made excuses for their children. The staff car arrived two hours later, and a pouty-faced Chloe flounced into my office. I had only begun to greet her when her parents pushed past the secretary to join us. Her mother, a petite woman, dressed in expensive workout wear, embraced her daughter and began to sob.

Oh my poor, poor girl!

Her father bellowed at me.

Give us some privacy! We need to talk to Chloe alone!

Not wanting to escalate an already volatile situation, I left them alone in my office.

I knocked on the door and entered the room after fifteen minutes. Chloe was slumped on her mother's lap, with her head resting on her mother's shoulder. Her father was sitting far away from them, seated behind my desk looking ready for battle. I felt myself bristle at the way he had intruded upon my personal working space. I moved to the conference table and suggested that we sit there together to review the situation.

I'll tell you the situation, yelled her father from behind my desk, seated in my chair. *My daughter was raped at camp, and your staff were negligent. I'm going to have this Hunter kid charged with rape. And you're going to get off your goddamn high horse and realize that I'm after your job.*

I sat down heavily in a chair at the conference room table.

Chloe, I began softly, *did you tell staff that you and Hunter were in love?*

Chloe shook her head and resettled against her mother.

Chloe, did you and Hunter plan to meet at night in your cabin?

What?! Her father interjected. *You blaming her for what happened? We're out of here!*

You might consider, I said, as they headed towards the door, *having Chloe checked out by her family doctor. And at some point, we should meet with Hunter and his parents to discuss what happened.*

They pushed past me in a furious rush. I sighed and waited for the next shoe to drop. Hunter and his parents would soon be arriving.

I retreated to my desk and was relieved to see that I had tucked away anything confidential before leaving the office earlier in the morning. No one really likes a bully, and even though I was the principal, I am no different. I understood that Chloe's parents were upset and that they were also processing the events, but their attack response rocked me a little and made me feel defensive and angry. I wanted the focus to be on Chloe and the reasons why she had responded in the way that she did. Her decision making, mistruths, and behaviour were potentially high risk and seemed to me to be a red flag of sorts. I wasn't sure what was motivating her, but the issue seemed to me something that was important.

I left my office to discover that Hunter and his father were calmly waiting for me. I ushered them in, and we sat down at the conference table. Greetings were briefly exchanged. Then, I began.

Hunter, I need you to walk us through everything that happened between you and Chloe at camp this weekend. Please don't leave anything out.

I'm sorry I broke the rules. But we didn't hurt anybody.

Hunter, you need to tell us what happened. We'll discuss rule breaking later.

Well... me and Chloe hooked up doing the high ropes. She was kinda' cute and seemed like way into me. We slipped away before dinner and went to the woods to be alone. And she was like pulling off my shirt and stuff and really getting into it...

And then?

And then she told me to come to her cabin at night, and she would show me something. She said she'd leave the door open a little, and so I went. I knew the rules, but she said she was just going to show me something, and I thought "how can that hurt?" I mean I was really into her by then.

Hunter's father interjected.

Is this really necessary? The kids broke the rules. Give them both detentions or whatever. Hunter shouldn't have to talk about this.

Actually, sir, with respect, it's important that we both hear all of what Hunter has to say. Chloe has accused Hunter of raping her. I'm trying to decide how best to respond, and I need to hear everything.

Fuck! No way! I did not. She fuckin' came after me. She was putting her hands down my pants the first time we were together, and she totally wanted to. But I didn't. I didn't cause I wasn't prepared; like, I didn't have a rubber. And she was all, "Oh come on baby. It won't matter once. I want you." And I was like, "no way, not taking a chance. Let's just cuddle." Then she like laughed at me. I don't fuckin' believe this.

Hunter put his head down on the table and began to sob. His father and I watched in a kind of shocked trance. After a couple of minutes, I stood up and gave Hunter a Kleenex box.

Mr. Terry, do you know a lawyer?

He nodded.

And then I suggest you go home and call him. I suggest you take Hunter to the police station and ask to speak to a youth officer. I'm going to call my contact there and give her a heads up. They'll be expecting you. It's important that Hunter makes a statement to the police while everything is still fresh and before anything else happens. Does this make sense?

He nodded.

C'mon son. We have to go now.

Hunter stood up and looked at me. His eyes reddened from crying, his face glistening with tears.

Miss, I've screwed up lots of times, and I screwed up again by going to the cabin, but it wasn't rape. Honest, it wasn't.

Shush, Hunter. No more talking. Go with your father. We'll talk again later.

I called my contact at the police station and did all of the other necessary Children's Aid reporting and documentation. This was going to be messy, and I needed to keep my notes in pristine order. Hunter was a skateboarder. He'd been in some minor difficulties in his junior years but had recently shown growth and maturity. He was well liked by staff, and I was pleased to see him take on a leadership role. His account of things seemed credible. I was fond of him but how could I not believe a girl who said she'd been raped? Chloe had been clear on that point. The stories didn't align very well.

The police took over the investigation and concluded, after several days of interviews, that they did not have anything that would warrant charges. Chloe had made a videotaped statement at the police station, but it was filled with inconsistencies and statements that did not correspond with witness accounts. She had refused services from the sexual assault crisis support team. Her family claimed that they were working with a private counsellor, *one of the best in the business*, they said.

I did not allow Chloe or Hunter to return to school until the situation was resolved and provided work for them to complete independently at home. In a large school full of teenagers, the rumours began to fly. Chloe texted her friends almost constantly, adding details to the stories and updates on her "rape trauma."

Once the police concluded their investigation, I allowed Hunter and Chloe to return to class but cautioned each to stay clear of the other with no further discussion about the events at camp. Hunter seemed relieved and eager to resume school. Chloe, by contrast, showed up looking timid and frightened and was hesitant to be separated from her mother. There was the usual gossip for a couple of days, but everything soon quieted down and school life continued.

Less than two weeks later, I was doing lunch supervision and walked into the gymnasium. Someone had just fallen to the floor from the top of the wooden bleachers. I rushed over and saw Chloe lying there, the wind knocked out of her. I used my walkie-talkie to call for backup and an ambulance.

Don't move, Chloe, I said. *Wait for the medics before you try to move.*

I can't feel my legs, she whispered.

Except for a small group who had witnessed the accident, we evacuated the gym while staff went out to meet the ambulance. The vice-principal called her parents and then began to interview the bystanders. The other students told us that Chloe had been walking along the top of the bleachers and had shouted *catch me* to one of the older boys. He was surprised by this and didn't know what she intended to do. She leapt from the top of the bleachers and landed in a heap on the floor. Chloe was now lying flat on her back, limbs perfectly outstretched like a starfish.

Who moved her? I shouted.

Her position looked unnatural for a fall. I was afraid that someone had touched her and potentially injured her. If she couldn't feel her legs, how did she arrange herself in a face-up starfish position? If she had jumped downwards, wouldn't she be face down on the floor?

The medics had by now arrived and were immobilizing her on a hard board.

No one moved her, Miss. She just fell on the floor in a mess like and then next thing you know she rolled like flat on the floor and was screamin' she couldn't feel her legs. And you were here then.

Did she lose consciousness at all? Blackout?

I scanned the small group quickly, searching for someone to provide answers. The group looked frightened. Students often had mishaps at school, but they were typically first-aid injuries. Paralysis was a whole new ballgame. I followed behind the medics as they carefully lifted Chloe, sandwiched on a board with blankets and multiple straps holding her firmly immobile, onto a stretcher and down the hall to the waiting ambulance.

Chloe's parents pulled up just as Chloe was being loaded and they rushed over to her.

What the hell happened?! yelled her father. *Chloe, baby, are you okay?* crooned her mother.

I can't feel my legs, said Chloe in response.

I saw the medics exchange a knowing look.

I'm going to fuckin' kill whoever did this, said her father. *And you*, he screamed, pointing at me, *I'm coming after you this time!* The ambulance pulled away, and her parents followed in their high-end car. I was frankly relieved to see them all leave.

My vice-principal had begun documenting and interviewing the bystanders when I returned to the building. Key details matched, without exception.

They were hanging out in the gym. Chloe climbed up the bleachers and was showing off on the top tier. A couple of students told her it wasn't safe and to get down. She shouted, "Catch me" to a senior boy. He looked up surprised, but she jumped at the same time, and he had no chance of catching her. She fell in a heap on the floor. She rolled herself out flat and then started screaming that she couldn't feel her legs. Then the principal walked in.

I readied myself for the telephone call in the evening. I was anxious to know how Chloe was while dreading yet another interaction with her father. The call was every bit as confrontational as anticipated. Her mother answered the phone and informed me that her husband had instructed her not to speak with me.

I'm sorry to hear that Mrs. Reinhardt, but I am concerned about Chloe and about you, actually, and just wanted a brief update.

She's at home with us. Tomorrow, we have to take her to see a neurologist for further testing.

So, her legs are fine?

I can't tell you anything else. She'll need more testing. She has many doctor's appointments lined up.

In the background, I heard her husband shouting.

Who the hell are you talking to?! Don't tell that fuckin' school a thing. I'm going to sue their asses off! They can all go to hell! Tell them to call our fuckin' lawyers!

The phone clicked and went dead.

A week later, I received a call from a law firm requesting a school transfer for Chloe. Transfers don't typically involve lawyers, but under the circumstances, I understood why they were involved. The paperwork was easily managed, and Chloe was set to begin class in a neighbouring school the following week. Schools are busy places, and we quickly resumed our routines. I wasn't sorry not to have to deal with Chloe's parents again.

Three weeks later, I received a call from the principal of the school where Chloe had transferred.

So, what can you tell me about Chloe? was the opener. *We have a situation here.*

Nice enough girl, average grades, lots of friends.

Can you tell me why she transferred mid-semester?

Her parents thought it would be in her best interest. They're not fans of this school or of me, in particular.

Why not?

She was involved in a situation at camp with a grade eleven boy. The police conducted an investigation, but there were no charges. Then, just before her transfer, she had a fall in the gym. Why are you asking?

Both of us had to be careful about our information exchange. Respecting student confidentiality is a serious matter and has to be balanced against safety issues that might help to provide care for a student.

We just found her in the backseat of a car with a senior. She was completely undressed and was lying on top of him. We knocked on the window to interrupt them. She dressed herself and came to the office. She claims the boy forced her.

Have you called her parents?

They're on their way.

I wasn't allowed to know what happened to Chloe, but I did worry about her. It was clear to me that three incidents in such a short interval were potentially indicative of something serious. She seemed to be deliberately engaging in attention-seeking, high-risk behaviours. Her father was the sort of man I instinctively disliked. He used his size, voice, and privilege to bully and intimidate. I assumed he did the same thing at home. His wife looked timid and deferential, not the sort who would likely tell him to cool his jets or calm down.

I have no clinical training and don't pretend to understand what was happening in Chloe's life. But the havoc she created seemed to me to be quite worrying. It was frightening to think of how vulnerable she would be if her behaviours continued. All I could hope was that at some point, her father would stop blaming others and realize that his daughter needed professional intervention and support before her safety, or the wellbeing of others, was further compromised.

Destiny

Every September, when the buses unload and the doors open, the halls fill with the energy and excitement of new and returning students. In the sea of faces that comprise a school population, it's sometimes possible to lose sight of individuals and see only a horde of young people moving en masse. In barely a week or two, idiosyncrasies become evident, and the separation between personalities becomes more distinct. As part of this process, I always tried to pay particular attention to the grade nines as they entered the building and worked to integrate themselves into the larger student population.

I remember Destiny clearly. She quickly established herself as a nurturer. Destiny was always the girl who amid adolescent drama would escort upset friends to the bathroom or the office. She was a pleaser, eager to be helpful in class and always the first to volunteer for anything. If you have ever watched a young foal stretching its legs and learning to run, you will have an idea of how Destiny moved. She was exceptionally tall and lanky compared to her peers, and her long legs and arms gave her an exuberant loose-limbed gait.

Academic work did not come easily to Destiny and, as a result, she was focussed and disciplined about her schoolwork. She took advantage of extra help, the resource room, and any other offers of assistance she was given. Unlike many students, she was not embarrassed about needing more help and was grateful for any extra assistance. She often spent lunch studying in the resource room or finishing homework in the library. It didn't take long before many of us on staff developed a real affection for her.

Destiny had three older brothers who were now working in the community. She also had a fourth brother who was only a couple of years older and was also a current student. The brothers who were out of school were known to be part of a wild group of heavy drinkers and were often mixed up in local crime. The fourth brother, Devin, was a naturally capable athlete but was undisciplined and uninterested in anything academic. His attendance was poor.

I commented to a guidance counsellor one day about how dissimilar Destiny and Devin seemed.

She's adopted, you know. Her mother wanted a girl and didn't want to risk having another boy.

Really?

Yeah. Her older brothers were enough of a handful. The oldest one is maybe twenty now, Doug. He's got a couple of kids already. The other two, Dawson and Dean, are in and out of jail. They all live at home, including Doug's girlfriend and the kids.

Oh wow. That must be a full house.

And not a big one either from the sounds of things. They don't have much. Dad is on welfare. Mom runs a daycare in the house.

Well, they're doing something right. Destiny is a great kid.

I agree. I just hope she gets a chance.

What do you mean?

So many people in one house, I worry about her. I suspect she does a lot of the childcare.

Well, families have to do what they can to make ends meet.

In contrast to Destiny, Devin was the kind of student who could drive any teacher crazy. He had a polite, if somewhat supercilious presentation, and could turn on the charm when he felt like it. He would bow his head in mock repentance when rebuked for absenteeism, lack of effort, or thoughtlessness. His friends seemed in thrall of him. They let him copy their answers during tests, they covered for his lack of participation during group assignments, and they lied about a long list of illnesses and misadventures that kept him from school. His parents also seemed equally enamoured of him and often harangued staff for not recognizing his potential and for being too hard on him.

When I took it upon myself to remonstrate with him, Devin shrugged his shoulders and scuffed his shoe on the floor, swinging it, pendulumlike, until black streaks from the sole of his shoe marked the floor and then faded with the repetition. His meek *yes m'am* was uttered with mock sincerity and frustrated my attempts to connect with him. Basketball was the only weapon in my arsenal, and I was loath to remove him from the team, knowing that it was the solitary aspect of school that truly engaged him.

When his parents trudged around the gym on parents' night, they were interested only in meeting with Devin's teachers. I would intercept them and attempt to guide them to Destiny's teachers as well, insisting that they hear how well she was doing at school and how highly the staff thought of her. They were only interested in complaining bitterly about their son's treatment at the hands of my staff.

At the end of grade ten, Destiny filled out her timetable for the following year, requesting a four-credit co-op. The school policy was to only allow four-credit work experiences to students who had completed their mandatory course load and were looking for specific skill development in preparation for apprenticeships or other workplace training. When the guidance staff met with her to explain this, she said that her parents were insisting on the four-credit option so she could stay home and help with babysitting. When asked if that was what she wanted to do, she slowly shook her head but would not speak.

Thus began my first real war with her parents. They attacked the guidance department staff first, accusing them of bias against Destiny and insisting that they were denying her the right to choose her own courses. This was ludicrous, of course, and when I finally intervened, they became even more aggressive. Among their many claims was that we were poverty shaming the family and had they been university graduates with fancy jobs and cars, we would allow them to do what they wanted. Destiny's father, in particular, was demanding, loud, and vulgar in his attacks. He called the local newspaper, the ministry, and the board in his campaign to undermine the school's decision. Finally, we were made to relent, and Destiny spent her first semester of grade eleven at home babysitting under the auspices of a co-op experience. It was a mockery of the program and a real disservice to her. Staff did what they could to provide enriching activities and monitored her carefully, but there was no way of disguising the abysmal misuse of the co-op program.

On those days when Destiny was in the building to cover the classroom components of the program, she seemed happy to be with her friends. On one such day, the students were completing mock job application, forms and Destiny told the teacher that she did not have a social insurance number because her parents would not let her apply for one. She further explained that her parents had told her a social insurance number was not necessary. She would continue to work at home and didn't need the government knowing everything about her. When pressed, Destiny admitted that she also did not have access to a copy of her birth certificate, and given the fact that she had been adopted, she had no way of applying for one. She became embarrassed by this when she realized that all of her friends had social insurance numbers and copies of their birth certificates.

It was the beginning of my second major conflict with her parents. With Destiny's permission, I called them to discuss the situation.

Whad-dya' want this time? was the rejoinder when I called the house.

I'd like to discuss an assignment that Destiny has to complete for her co-op credit.

She not doin' everything she's supposed to?

Yes, she is. She's trying to. But there's a small problem.

And what would that be?

She needs to complete some mock job application forms and we have discovered that she doesn't have a social insurance number. She needs one to apply for jobs and other things, and we would like her to apply for one.

She don't need it.

It was clear that her mother was holding a crying baby, and I was certain that she had deliberately placed the speaker near the wailing child.

Well, actually, she does.

Look. You said these applications were mock or whatever. So, give her a mock number and get off my ass. I've got more important shit to do!

And then the phone was hung up.

Destiny was in my office when I made the call, and her mother's voice was loud enough for her to hear both sides of the conversation. When I looked at her, I saw that she was wiping away tears and trying to smile at me.

Thank you for trying, Miss. I'm sorry she was rude to you.

It broke my heart to hear this sweet girl apologizing for her mother's behaviour, but there was nothing else I could do for her. I smiled weakly in response and tried to say something encouraging. Destiny excused herself and slipped away, looking embarrassed by the situation.

A week or so later, Devin's father called me. He was in a rage because, as he wrongly insisted, Devin had not been issued a mid-term report card. He wanted to know why his son was being denied a report card and expressed himself in the most colourful language. I interrupted his rant long enough to pull up a digital copy of the document and offered to read the marks and comments to his father. It was clear to me that Devin had not been at school when the reports were issued and had not bothered to collect the document at the office when he returned. The marks weren't good; he was failing all four of his classes. The number of days absent for each class was actually higher than the marks he had earned. The comments included: "must attend regularly if he wishes to earn the credit" and "must complete all outstanding assignments if he wishes to pass."

His father remained furious. He wanted to know why the teachers weren't making allowances for Devin's headaches and stress-related illnesses. According to his father, Devin was a really bright student with a group of terrible teachers who didn't support him. I offered to set up some parent-teacher interviews, but indicated that without medical documentation, we could not simply ignore the pattern of absenteeism. This comment launched another volley of profanity and abuse and ended when he hung up the phone.

Thus began my renewed conflict with the family that erupted in bursts of profanity and threats directed towards me and included phone calls of complaint to my superiors at the board office. After several days of heated verbal abuse, I was finally able to meet with Devin, his parents, and his teachers to sort out a plan. Everything was dependent upon Devin's willingness to attend school regularly, actively participate in class, and complete core assignments. A guidance teacher would monitor his progress and provide his parents with weekly updates.

Devin was meek and compliant during the meeting and seemed somewhat intimidated by the presence of his parents. I was surprised to see the respectful way in which he addressed them. I hoped rather than believed that this might be the end of our conflict. And although Devin's morning attendance did improve, he often did not return in the afternoons, regularly disappearing with his friends at lunch. His assignments began to be handed in, however, and he slowly began to earn some passing marks. But issues remained.

One of his teachers brought me a homework assignment of Devin's to look at. The handwriting was a dead giveaway. It had all of the rounded loops and carefully shaped letters of Destiny's penmanship, complete with the odd happy face marking the end of a page. Devin's careless scrawl bore no resemblance to this writing. It was clear that he was passing his work on to his sister and she was doing her best to help him get through the pile of outstanding assignments. Destiny, as I have said, was not a naturally gifted student, and this must have been exacting work for her and would have taken considerable extra effort.

I called home and invited the parents in to meet with me and to review Devin's remarkable improvement. Although they were suspicious, they came in. Devin brazenly claimed the work as his own. His parents defended him. We were at a stalemate: The parents claimed that the school was out to get Devin, and I was irritated to no end by their deception and their abuse of Destiny. With no way to prove what we all knew to be obvious, Devin scraped by and was awarded three of the credits with marks in the low fifties.

Destiny returned for second semester, and although she slipped into her friend group easily, we all noticed a distinct change to her disposition. She often looked troubled. Her sweet good nature seemed clouded by worries, and she was no longer the first to volunteer or jump into something new. Staff tried to suss out what was worrying her, but she remained guarded and would not disclose her troubles.

At the end of grade eleven, Destiny once more asked for a four-credit co-op. She still had a number of mandatory course requirements to fulfill, and I denied the request. I pointed out the necessity for her to complete math and English credits before I could consider another co-op experience. I fully expected another scene with her parents and dreaded a rehash of our last conflict. Instead, to my relief and surprise, the phone calls did not come. There was complete silence from the family as we finished out the year.

The following August, as we were preparing to open school, Devin showed up and requested a four-credit co-op. He wanted to work in his parents' daycare. He indicated that he was intending to become an early childhood educator and that this would be good preparatory experience. I didn't even pretend to argue.

When school started in the fall, Destiny looked gaunt. Her once soft features now looked sharp. There was clearly something troubling her, and whatever it was had become worse over the summer months. I asked one of the guidance teachers to approach her to see if she would agree to speak with the visiting nurse practitioner and was glad to hear that she had agreed to do so.

A couple of weeks later, Destiny appeared in my office and asked if she and the guidance teacher could speak to me about something legal. When they both came in a few minutes later, I was shocked to hear that Destiny wanted to become an emancipated minor and apply for student welfare. She wanted my assistance with the process.

May I ask why?

Because of Devin and my parents. They make me do things.

What sorts of things, Destiny?

Well, babysitting all the time so I can never go out with my friends and cooking dinner every night and doing all the laundry. That's one thing. But then there's other stuff too.

Can you tell me?

Well, you already know some of it. Devin's school work and stuff. There's more.

I waited quietly to see if she would continue.

Devin isn't really my brother, you know. I'm adopted.

I know, honey.

So, my parents said it was okay.

Said what was okay?

What he does to me. And my other brothers laugh and don't stop him. They all treat me like trash.

What does Devin do, Destiny? Can you tell me?

He uses me for sex and stuff and makes me do things. He pulls my hair and forces me. I never feel safe when he's home...

Do your parents know?

They won't do anything. They say it's okay because I'm adopted.

I was horrified by the revelation.

My God, Destiny. It's not okay. You know that, don't you?

She shrugged her shoulders and looked at me, scrutinizing my face.

I guess...

We should call the police.

No! My parents will kill me.

Have they threatened you?

She nodded silently.

What did they say?

She became quite emotional and answered me between her sobs.

They said I was a liar... and... even... even... if... it was true... nobody would care... and... that Devin was a... good boy... and urges... urges were natural.

Destiny, we can't let you live like this. No one should be treated like this. We need to find you a safe place to go.

I was furious. Destiny had been trembling and gulping, but now she also began to cry deep wracking sobs as she released some of her unhappiness. I waited until she began to compose herself and passed her handfuls of tissue. The guidance counsellor was sitting beside her and had been patting her back and comforting her gently. When she was cried out, I asked her again, *May I call the police?*

No!

What would you like us to do? How can we help you?

I want to get away. To live on my own. I don't want Devin to ever touch me. I need a job, and I can't get one because I don't have any identification.

I looked at the guidance staff member, and our eyes locked. We were both horrified and desperate to find a way through the mess.

Do you have a friend? Somewhere safe where you can stay until all of this gets sorted?

Destiny thought for a minute.

Maybe Kate. Her parents are nice. They might let me stay. They have a big house.

The remainder of the day was spent making arrangements for a short-term respite space for Destiny. I contacted a social services case worker who prioritized a file for her. They ultimately contacted her parents and demanded a copy of her birth certificate. Having met the parents, social services expedited student welfare. Parents of a friend offered to rent her a bedroom in their home. Destiny did not want the police involved. As a result, Devin was never charged for multiple sexual assaults, and her parents were never held accountable.

Destiny finished her high school diploma, left town, and began a modelling career. Modelling was something she really wanted to do. I think she saw it as a glamorous way of life. A caring guidance counsellor and a compassionate social services worker rescued Destiny from her situation. I remain deeply grateful for the work of such skilled individuals even as I continue to wonder about her, praying that she is somewhere safe.

Jasmine

A high school is always a microcosm of the larger community. This includes all of the socioeconomic demographics as well as a cross-section of values. Racial and sexual slurs and epithets are strictly forbidden in schools. Jasmine, a new grade ten student, was being taunted regularly and routinely. The hateful words were called out loudly in halls filled with teenagers pushing their way to class and also quietly in hate-filled whispers when they were near to her. Anyone caught using such language was subject to strict school discipline, and all the students knew this. But still, it continued, subversively and destructively. Day after day, Jaz appeared in my office, teary and indignant. How she withstood the barrage, I still do not know.

We tried to do everything right. We celebrated many religious and cultural holidays. We in-serviced the staff and the leadership group on equity, racism, gender identity, and human rights. We promoted inclusion and acceptance and positive mental health. We consulted with experts, read books, attended workshops, disciplined the worst offenders, brought in the police, and facilitated restorative conferences. Yet the ugliness continued. Jaz was the sole targeted victim. She was also the sole visible minority in a school filled with shades of white. Her friends attempted to cushion her from the hate-filled comments but the slurs were razor-sharp and cut deeply.

I worried about the impact on her of such relentless animosity. In desperation, I invited her family in to discuss the matter with me. I was shocked when she finally led her two very white parents into my office.

I'm adopted, she shrugged, looking at me.

I attempted to recover my composure and got right to business.

I'm worried about Jasmine's self-esteem. You know we are attempting to combat some terrible racial slurs, but I'm afraid that they're having an impact. I have tried every possible approach I know to resolve this issue, and now I'm seeking some suggestions from you as to how I might better support your daughter.

Her father, a well-dressed man in his early forties, leaned forwards earnestly and smiled at me.

The truth is, she's going to have to live with it. Our society is racist. Jasmine knows she is loved for who she is and beyond that, she has to cope with the bullshit. We can't protect her from it.

Look, you're a nice lady. You've tried. We've talked many times about what you are trying to do here. It's up to Jasmine to walk proud, hold her head up, and prove to these idiots that she's better than they are. It's what we teach her to do.

Jasmine, I said, looking at her directly, is there anything you have to add? Is there anything you can think of that would help?

I just want to be done with school. I hate it here. Maybe a school where there are more kids like me?

That's possible. There are schools I know that have a more mixed student population. Although there wouldn't be bussing. You would need a drive.

That's not possible, interjected her father. She can't run away from her problems. Her mother and I both work. We can't drive her.

Could you drop her close to a bus stop on your way to work? I could make arrangements for her to attend any number of schools close to your route.

How would she get home? No! We don't want to teach her this. She has to stand up and face things.

With respect, Mr. and Mrs. Stevenson, it's hard to stand up for things when you feel like you're standing alone.

I was angry. With possibly the best intentions in the world, they seemed unable to step outside of their privilege to understand what it was they were requiring of their teenage daughter. Her love for them would not allow her to hurt them by revealing the full extent of the ugliness she was experiencing.

Her parents were intractable. Jasmine's shoulders drooped. She looked down at the floor, deflated. I felt ill and powerless. A few days later, Jasmine appeared at school wearing a wig. It was a very chic bob, cut with flat, straight hair in a light blonde colour. Hidden was the riot of soft black hair that typically framed her face. She continued wearing the wig. I wondered what her motivation was but did not engage her in a conversation. I did not then appreciate the repeated microaggressions she experienced when people reached out to pat the soft black fuzz of her natural hair.

A month or so later, she showed up wearing a second wig. This one was blue-black and was styled in an angled bob with full puffed-out hair. She walked down the hall like a runway model, hips swaying confidently, head held high, friends surrounding her. Somehow, I thought, the wigs were giving her confidence. I noticed that she switched back and forth between the two wigs until a third one appeared. The third one was an elaborate piece that reached part way down her back and was comprised of dozens and dozens of tiny braids in a reddish-brown colour. The braids were twisted and looped together in an elegant fashion statement. I saw her girlfriends patting it and making admiring noises. The effect of the hairpieces had somehow subverted some of the racist chatter. I hoped that the worst was over and the offenders had grown weary of their target.

Unfortunately, it was not to be. A couple of days later, Jaz and her friends appeared in my office with a list of boys who had made disparaging and racist commentary. Included on the list were the names of two staff members who had heard the verbal assaults and not addressed the situation. The girls were furious and demanded I take immediate action. I disciplined the boys. I called their parents. I brought in the police to caution the boys. And I registered the teachers for a professional development opportunity on equity.

In her grade eleven year, we were able to place Jaz in a high school/college program. It was an elite opportunity allowing students to attend college while earning high school and college credits. She registered for a cosmetology/hairdressing elective and attended college three days a week. In the remaining two days a week, Jaz still had to attend high school. Despite all of my efforts, I suspected that when she walked down the hallway, someone would still whisper hate. I came to understand that the biases and values reinforced in some homes were poisoning our efforts within the school. And that Jaz continued to suffer.

Rachel

It was late June, and I had a scheduled intake appointment with a new student and her father. Rachel was joining a special needs class in our school, and I understood that she did not want the placement. She had been fully integrated throughout her elementary career and had been age promoted with her peers, despite severe cognitive impairments.

A timid-looking man and his daughter were ushered into my office at the appointed time. Rachel wore heavy makeup and an elaborate hairstyle that involved glittery hairspray and multiple scrunchies. She was wearing tight-fitting, high-fashion clothing and expensive running shoes. She looked every inch the image of a teen pop star. Frankly, I was impressed. I fingered her student file on my desk, but left it closed. I wondered, just for a few seconds, if the school had misdiagnosed her and underestimated her potential. I had carefully reviewed the medical documents inside, including the testing reports and a psychological services summation. All of those professionals could not be mistaken. Still, I looked at her with wonder.

Welcome to your new school! I hope you will be happy here and make lots of new friends.

Her father smiled at me, but Rachel did not.

I already have friends! And I want to be with them!

She pouted at me. I suspected it was a look that worked on her father. I heard a slight speech impediment when she spoke. The left side of her face had been carefully covered with a thick coating of foundation and a curtain of hair. Her bright purple lipstick, though well applied, showed a slight twist to her mouth.

Well Rachel, that's why we're here today. We're going to discuss how to make sure you have a good experience while also learning some of the things that you need to know.

I just want to be with my friends! I don't care about anything else!

Again, the pout. Her little chin tipped out, her bottom lip projecting outwards on a slight angle. Her speech impediment was even more discernable. Her father shifted in his seat uncomfortably. He looked helpless.

Rachel, it's my job to make sure you receive an education. I want to help you find a balance between those things you would like to do and those things that you need to do. Because that's part of what being an adult means: accepting responsibility and becoming responsible for yourself. No adult that I know gets to do what they want all the time. I bet your dad doesn't get to do what he wants all the time. Do you?

I looked pointedly at her father, trying to draw him into the conversation.

He shrugged his shoulders in response and said, *Rachel, you need to listen to this lady. She knows what she's talking about.*

I had previously arranged for the support team to join me after a few minutes of private chat, and they appeared at the door on cue. Together, we were able to build Rachel a timetable that kept her in a special needs class for the majority of the day but allowed her to reverse integrate with her friends for gym in first semester and art in second semester. She would also be allowed to have an unsupervised lunch in the cafeteria. It was an excellent compromise, and I was excited we had arrived at a customized solution for her. Rachel was not happy, however, and burst into tears of frustration part way through our meeting. She was inconsolable, and although her father tried to calm her down, she continued to escalate into a full-blown tantrum.

In September, Rachel arrived at school on the bus with her friends. They proceeded to their lockers and classrooms while Rachel wandered back and forth in the front hallway. She was furious when I approached and asked if she wanted me to walk with her to her classroom.

I fuckin' hate—hate—hate you! she screamed. *You're fuckin' ruining my life!*

Her screams echoed in the space and brought a number of staff running to see what was going on. We escorted her outside and allowed her to shriek and scream until she wore herself out. Then she meekly followed one of the teachers to her classroom.

Things did not progress very well for Rachel that day. She refused to be seated at a desk and threw her backpack at the teacher. She paced at the back of the classroom and continued to mutter and swear at the educational assistants trying to comfort her. She created an ongoing disruption and upset the other students in the room who were also new and trying to acclimatize. When the lunch bell sounded, she grabbed her backpack and found her own way to the cafeteria where she waited for friends.

Rachel had not anticipated the vast numbers of students in the school and wandered up and down the cafeteria aisles looking for people she knew. By the time the lunch period was over, she still had not sat down or opened her lunch. It was an incredibly painful situation to watch unfold. We sent an educational assistant to find her, and she eventually convinced Rachel to return to the classroom to eat something.

It took several weeks for Rachel to become resigned to her new schedule. What became clear to the adults in the building was that her elementary school friends were meeting new students and forming new relationships. Although they included Rachel when she joined them, they did not seek out her company. Rachel was also struggling to keep up with them in their shared gym class. She had sustained a shattered pelvis in a car accident some years before and as a result moved stiffly and with limitations. Although her teacher attempted to include her in all activities, she was often the last to be chosen for any team.

In her own classroom, Rachel rebuffed all offers of friendship and refused to join in class activities. She insisted that her desk be kept apart from the other students and that she be given independent work to complete. We all believed that with time and patience, she would engage and participate. We did not anticipate her stubborn nature or her strong conviction that she was being wronged by all of us.

Academically, Rachel was low functioning. She could print her name and recognize some familiar words in a level-one reader, but she had no concept of money, counting, or basic math skills. Any learning that she worked on one day would seem entirely new to her on the next. Her executive skills were also problematic. She was constantly misplacing her shoes, papers needing signatures, and gym uniform. She refused to use a locker, preferred to stuff her belongings into her backpack, and carried her coat with her everywhere.

And then, suddenly, Rachel found a boyfriend a month into term. He was a grade eleven student and was smitten by her pop-star clothes, hair, and makeup. In no time, they were seen walking the halls together and holding hands before school and at lunch. We watched their courtship with a mixture of relief and trepidation.

On the night of the first school dance, Rachel arrived in an excited state with some of her girlfriends. She looked sensational in spikey-heeled shoes and a form-fitting mini-dress. Her boyfriend arrived separately, and they were soon together, enjoying the chocolate fountain and watching the dancing. Early in the evening, however, her boyfriend left abruptly with some of his friends. I saw Rachel wandering around on her own again but didn't think much about it. Later, I heard from staff that someone had told the boy that Rachel was in the slow class and that he was a loser for hanging out with her.

Rachel texted him for days afterwards and followed him around the school until she finally lost hope. Her broken heart complicated her despondency, and she resumed her outbursts and shouted profanities. None of us were exempt from her rage, as she threw things at will and swore at all of us. We consulted with her specialists but were told that the outbursts had happened since the accident and were not likely to be subdued. Some felt that expressing her frustration and rage this way was not entirely unreasonable.

Although we allowed Rachel to walk to class and the cafeteria unsupervised, she was always accompanied to the bus at the end of the day. The parking lot was busy, and we needed to ensure she remained safe and boarded the right bus. It became a challenge for her to evade the educational assistant chaperoning her and run to join the throng of students waiting for the buses to load. It was worrisome behaviour, and although we tried to reason with her, we could not persuade her to comply. Dismissal time became an all-out chase, as several of us attempted to catch up with her to guide her to the correct lineup. For our efforts, we were all rewarded with Rachel screaming, *Leave me the fuck alone!*

One afternoon, a woman claiming to be Rachel's mother showed up at the school. She was dressed in a full-length mink coat, with impeccable hair and makeup. When I went to shake her hand, I smelled booze. It wasn't a mouthwash smell but a boozy stench wafting from her skin and clothing.

I'm here to pick up my daughter. I'll take her for dinner and drive her home afterwards. She said this loftily, breezily, as if it were the most natural thing in the world.

I'll have to call her father first. I understand he has full custody.

She'll want to see me. I've been away, you see, and haven't seen her for some time.

Still, let me phone him. You're welcome to have a seat and wait.

The dismissal bell rang while I was looking up the phone number. Rachel's mother swept out of my office and disappeared. I completed the call and discovered there was a restraining order in place and that Rachel's mother was not to have any access. I rushed outside to the bus and collided with a hysterical Rachel who was running back into the building, shrieking and sobbing.

I saw her... I saw her... were the only words I could make out.

Your mother? Did you see your mother, Rachel?

She's NOT my mother!

The woman in the fur coat? Who is she?

The one who ruined my life! I should be dead!

I held her in my arms until the sobbing subsided, and then I called her father again and asked him to collect her. I dispatched a staff member to see if the woman in the fur coat was still lingering on the property. I was careful not to ask Rachel any further questions lest I upset her again. Her father showed up in good time, and a quieted but still distraught Rachel burrowed into him while he embraced her and kissed the top of her head. When she was calmer, he asked her to wait outside my office while he spoke with me in private.

During our brief conversation, he informed me that Rachel's mother had been driving the car when she lost control and crashed. Three of their children were in the backseat. None were wearing seatbelts. His ex-wife had been driving drunk and had hit a light standard. Rachel had been the most severely hurt, but all three children suffered serious injuries. Rachel's cognitive impairment was the cruellest blow, as she was still able to remember snatches of life before the accident, along with the multiple surgeries she had endured and the years of physiotherapy. Her mother had been sentenced to a short stay in prison, and he had filed for divorce and custody. Initially, she had been given limited access but had returned the children one day while clearly under the influence and with all three children retraumatized. Hence the restraining order.

She was a beautiful woman, but she can't leave the booze alone. We were a happy family once.

So Rachel's misery and deep unhappiness were finally explained. And I understood for the first time that our little pop-star diva was paying the price for someone else's crime in a way that would shadow her life forever.

Alex

Ours was a school at some distance from the nearest major city. Located in a rural community, we were surrounded by prosperous family farms. Many of the boys wore cowboy boots with tight jeans and large decorative belt buckles. The older students drove their trucks to school, and among the mud-covered pick-ups that arrived every morning were three jacked-up monster trucks that sported the Confederate flag prominently pinned in the rear window. My vice-principal was vigilant about the offensive flags, and the boys soon learned to stop outside the parking lot to unfasten the flag before entering the school parking lot. At the end of the day, they would park on the adjacent side street and refasten them. This was a hard-won standoff position.

A very small, almost secretive, Gay-Straight Alliance (GSA) group met at the school on an infrequent basis. The numbers varied between six and ten regulars with the occasional drop-in member. The meetings were not broadcast over the public address system, and invitations were by word of mouth only. Ours was a conservative community, and, unfortunately, there were even members of the teaching staff who made the group feel unwelcome. At the same time that this small group was struggling to survive, we had an active student council with over thirty regular participants.

Hosting a GSA in high schools had become a provincial requirement for all publicly funded schools. It wasn't a popular decision among a particular demographic in our community, and I was frequently challenged by parents who took personal affront to the idea of such a group. Parents regularly sidled up to me and conspiratorially asked a variation of the following question: *So how do you really feel about these homos meeting in your school?*

When I assured them that I was entirely supportive of the group, I was pointedly asked: *Would you happen to be a church-going woman?*

After my response in the affirmative, a follow-up question came next: *Now does your reverend know what it is you're allowing in the school?*

Despite some parental discord, creating a safe and welcoming environment for all students was my priority. I casually suggested to student council one day that they might consider inviting the GSA group to participate in their planning. The students greeted the idea enthusiastically, and within the week, Alex was invited to be the liaison between the GSA and student council. Alex attended both meetings and quickly became a dynamic leader. Her newly minted profile, however, necessitated a personal disclosure she had not yet made known. She came out as gay to her family and friends, creating small shock waves.

To those people who knew Alex well, the announcement was a confirmation rather than a surprise. She had chosen to identify as one of only two openly gay students in the building. Some name-calling took place but then seemed to quieten down as other dramas played out. Several of us kept a close watch on Alex to ensure she was not being bullied. Alex, for her part, was pretty resilient; she had a steely will and a positive attitude. She was an excellent student who had applied to several university programs. Initially, at least, all indications were she was managing well.

Gradually as the semester played out, Alex began to alter her appearance. Shifting from black goth outfits and heavy eyeliner, she began to sport a more androgynous, gender-neutral wardrobe. She shaved her hair off and stopped wearing any makeup. She appeared to favour loose-fitting, oversized clothes and thickly soled shoes. It was a fairly dramatic alteration, but it suited her and seemed to be purposeful. It may have been this rapid transformation that garnered the attention of some of the boys.

I began to hear from staff and other students that the cowboys were giving Alex a hard time. They wolf whistled at her in the hallway. They muttered *lesbo* under their breath when they passed her in the cafeteria. Although they were reprimanded and cautioned, they continued to escalate their torment. LESBO was scratched into her locker door one morning. Another time glue was smeared over her lock making it impossible to open. Her backpack was kicked across the classroom and stomped on. In the computer lab, a picture of Alex was emailed to all the school computers with a message indicating that she was available for free blow jobs. The onslaught was unremitting.

I spoke to each of the boys we suspected, and they all blithely denied having done any of these things, demanding that I prove it was them. I called their homes and explained to their parents that the activities were bordering on hate crimes and I needed their assistance to communicate the message to their sons, or I would call the police in to investigate. Although I was not given any assurances by the parents, the calls must have had some impact because no new incidents were reported.

Believing that the storm had passed, I encouraged the GSA to expand their group and welcome allies to their meetings. The group quickly grew to sixty members, and they began to meet on a biweekly basis, coordinating their activities with the student council. I was delighted to see the wide cross-section of students attending the group and continued to encourage them when I had the opportunity. They gave away rainbow-coloured cupcakes as part of an awareness campaign and quietly advocated for further support on gender-based issues within the school community and beyond.

At the same time that these activities were quietly taking place, Alex was struggling with a much more intense conflict on the home front. Apparently, both of her parents were upset about her having become public about her sexuality and had suggested that "*the feelings she was having*" might be temporary. Out of a surfeit of caring, they tried to communicate that keeping her sexuality under wraps might be in her best interest. Alex did not view their position as supportive, and this was creating some intense emotions on both sides.

I received a telephone call one morning from a local business owner. Alex was a part-time employee there and the manager wanted me to know what had happened the previous night. Alex had shown up after school for a shift. A group of six boys had followed her inside and had begun to quietly heckle and jeer at her. One of them was overheard telling his friends that he was *going to give her a good fuck so she would know what she was missing*. A friend responded with, *Ya'. That's right. We should all do her.*

A horrified customer had alerted the manager, who called the police. The quick-thinking manager took Alex out the backdoor and drove her home in his car. The police had informally cautioned the boys but hadn't charged them. The manager was sure that Alex could tell me the names of the boys involved.

I was incensed at the news and also worried for Alex's safety. I spoke to her later that morning and she identified the boys. As I suspected, the group was almost entirely made up of the same "cowboys" who had formerly harassed her at school. Parent interviews were scheduled for later in the week, and I waited a couple of days, knowing that the boys' parents would be coming to the school. I started with Chris's parents, as I believed he was the group's leader. His parents were typically pleasant, and I had had several positive conversations with them.

On parents' night, I circulated among the crowds and stayed on the alert, looking for Chris's parents. They entered the gym near the end of the evening and progressed across the room slowly, greeting friends and acquaintances. Mrs. Petty was a petite, delicate-looking woman, nicely dressed and someone who had once been quite beautiful. She carried herself with a certain air of grace, with hands that fluttered at her side and a demure smile that was meant to charm. Her husband seemed to dominate her in every way. He was tall, permanently wind or sunburned, and broad shouldered, with a loud, boisterous voice. His strides were long and forceful, and he filled the space with his personality. He was wearing an expensive lambskin jacket, jeans, and cowboy boots made with exotically patterned leather, tipped with pointed metal toe caps. I knew him to be a respected local figure.

I invited the pair into my office for a quick chat, and they obligingly followed me. I had a whole speech prepared in my head and was about to launch into it when a brief flash of light hit Mr. Petty's belt buckle as he leaned back in his chair. Distracted momentarily, I looked at the buckle for a few seconds until I realized what it was. Silver edges formed the backing for an enamelled version of the Confederate flag. Mr. Petty saw me staring and made a show of hooking his thumb into the belt so that the rest of his hand rested prominently beside the flag. He waved his hand up and down in a subtle flapping motion while I watched.

Mr. Petty, you know that the Confederate flag is not welcome on school property.

I paused.

And I really need your support with Chris. I'm told the police had to speak with him a few nights ago. Did he tell you about that?

Go on.

My understanding is that he was threatening to rape a girl, and while I'm not suggesting that he actually intended to carry through on that, you have to make him understand that those are not things that people can joke about.

And my understanding, Miss, is that the girl in question wasn't much of a looker. He'd a been doin' her a favour from what I heard. And this buckle here, it's on my property, and not yours.

I was stunned and angry. I took a breath before responding.

I don't want to argue with you about details. I'm simply asking you to let Chris know that he has to stop taunting this girl, or it's going to turn into a criminal matter. She has the right to be safe at school, and it's my job to see that she is.

He nodded at me curtly, sucked his teeth slowly in an elaborate show of distaste, and strode out of the office without the usual courtesies. His wife followed behind at a more genteel pace but without making eye contact or acknowledging that she had even heard the conversation. I was frustrated. How on earth could I hope to challenge Chris's behaviour when it was so obviously being reinforced at home? *The apple doesn't fall far from the tree* is the line that people always reference when discussing such situations. But I believed it was possible to collect those apples and toss them just a little further out. I had to believe that because I saw it as part of my job—to expose young people to a broader way of thinking and help them become responsible social citizens. Citizenship is one of the key responsibilities of schooling. People often forget that.

I slammed some files around on my desk and tried to calm myself before rejoining the rest of the parents and staff. I didn't, in all honesty, feel like having any more challenging conversations that night. Instead, I worked my way through the crowd, smiling and nodding at those I knew, and avoiding further serious dialogue. Although I often enjoyed parent-teacher night, I couldn't wait to announce that there were only five minutes left before closing. Staff were tired and needed to get home, and I wanted desperately to get away. The interaction had left me feeling a little contaminated and soiled. I just wanted to scrub off my makeup and pull on something clean and comfy. I kept imagining the smirk on Chris's face when his father told him about our meeting. The story would quickly spread.

Despite my perceived ineffectiveness, Chris kept a low profile after I met with his parents. Alex's behaviour, however, became worrying. She began to miss class, and her grades dropped accordingly. The work she handed in, when she actually appeared in school, was shoddy and nowhere near her usual standard. Although she had applied to university, it became clear that she needed to change her behaviours if she wanted to improve her average. Staff spoke to her, offered her support, and gave her lots of leeway, but Alex did not respond to their concern.

We heard rumours of her drinking heavily at parties on the weekend and getting completely wasted. She stopped socializing with her friends at school and started commuting to the city on weekends for parties with new friends. Stories of her drinking and reckless hookups were numerous. Sightings of her waiting at the bus stop during the school day were mentioned, as well as the occasional story from someone who had seen her throwing up on the street. She was fired from her job. As Alex unravelled, so too did our GSA. She had been the driving force behind their energy. and without her, they were dispirited.

Our guidance department staff tried to counsel her on occasion when she did show up at school, but she was unwilling to talk about what was going on in her life. When asked about her parents, she dismissed them as useless and a joke and wouldn't allow the school to call them. Alex was by this time eighteen, and we had no legitimate way of intervening in her spiral. We could only watch as she continued to self-medicate and self-destruct. It was appalling to see someone in such awful pain and not be able to help in any kind of impactful way. I wondered if by encouraging her to become a leader, we had unintentionally set in motion exposure to the cruel forces that broke her.

The last I heard, she planned to take a gap year and then maybe do community college. She moved away from home and was working in the city somewhere. The GSA group didn't recover, attendance dwindled down to three or four, and they once again became secretive about the timing and location of their meetings. I knew that it would take several years for all of us to get past the ugliness and rebuild trust.

Tia

On our way home from the city one night, my partner and I stopped at an all-night grocery store to pick up some bread and fruit for breakfast. I had intended to do the grocery shopping earlier, but the day got away from me, and before I knew it, we were rushing off to dinner and the symphony. It was nearly midnight, and we were ridiculously overdressed for a late-night shopping trip: me in a floor-length gown and my partner in a formal suit. The store was unfamiliar, and we wandered up and down the aisles looking for the bakery section. Out of the corner of my eye, I saw a vaguely familiar figure dart away from me. Curious, I followed and saw her deliberately evade me once again. At the far end of the next aisle, I finally caught a good look at her. Although it was winter, she had bare feet in flip-flops, a pair of men's oversized grey track pants, and a filthy ski jacket. As I turned down the aisle, I saw her stuffing items down the front of her jacket. She was with a young man, fairly tall, who was also poorly dressed for the weather, and she seemed to be instructing him. Both were busy filling their jackets with tins of fruit and soup.

She saw me looking at her and whispered something to her partner while giggling. He turned to look at me—a long, steady gaze filled with curiosity and challenge. I knew that she recognized me. They ran down the aisle and out of the store. I made no attempt to call after them or to report them to the clerks. There was no point. They had already disappeared into the murky night. And just like that, my carefree evening ended, and I was flooded with memories of the girl and all of our abortive attempts to help her.

Her name was Tia, a fetal alcohol syndrome child whose mother's approach to morning sickness was to get drunk. Tia's mother admitted to drinking heavily throughout her pregnancy, not believing any of the stories about alcohol harming the baby. Tia was the result: a volatile young girl with small eyes, an upturned snub nose, a thin upper lip, and severe learning disabilities. At fifteen, she could not read, tell time, or print her name. Her short-term memory and ability to focus seemed nonexistent. Abstract reasoning, impulse control, and basic life skills were also deficient. Personal care like grooming and hygiene was also a challenge. She disliked baths and showers, stating that the water hurt her skin. On occasion, she had been seen wearing jeans crusted with menstrual blood. Her temper was a force to be reckoned with. She could throw furniture and completely destroy a classroom in under five minutes. I had learned to safely evacuate the other students in the room and let her rage until she wore herself out. There was no way of stopping her once the adrenaline was pumping. And here she was, north of the city, in the dead of night, stealing groceries.

Tia and school did not mix, and she knew this far better than the rest of us. I believed that we simply had to find the right program for her. All previous attempts to integrate her into a school had failed. We tried full-time, part-time, and once-a-week schedules, only to have her show up at school and explode in frustration part way through her first class. We brought in support teams, counsellors and coaches who attempted to work one-on-one with her, but Tia did not connect with any of them. An educational advocate sent by Children's Aid insisted that the school system had failed her and that we needed to do more to help her. They paid for an intervention specialist to attend class with her for two hours a week only. Tia was embarrassed by the *bullshit babysitter* and ran away to hide in the stairwell. Trapped there like a feral cat, she snapped and snarled at us until we finally withdrew and allowed her to escape out of doors.

The sensory room failed when she slammed the bean bag chair so hard that the seam burst, spilling its stuffing throughout the small room. Gym class was a disaster, as she refused to engage in team sports, shower, or change. Art was no better. She threw clay at the other students. And in the computer room when she became frustrated, she pushed a short row of computer monitors off the table onto the floor. We failed to create a win for her in any of the places where we usually had success. Instead, she repeatedly slipped away from staff and made her way to the smoking area to bum cigarettes and joints from anyone there.

Socializing with the other students who hated school and who could often be found slinking around the smoking area was the only normative behaviour we ever saw her engaged in. Having been age promoted through elementary school, Tia's inability to read created huge barriers in her grade nine program. Although we attempted to have her work with our special-education teacher on a reading recovery program, Tia refused to do *fuckin' baby crap* and threw books and binders at the staff member, overturned the furniture, and screamed loudly, smashing her own head against the walls until she finally ripped open the office door and ran outside.

During her two years at high school, she failed to complete a single assignment, test, or course credit. Her absences far exceeded the number of times she was present. We could not find an alternative program to meet her needs and the programming available at our school was far too challenging for her. Her classroom behaviour was so volatile and disruptive that other students were frightened of her, and staff members were wary and unwilling to be alone with her. It was a sad and troubling state of affairs.

We learned at one point that Tia had connected with someone in the smoking area, a designated space at the edge of our property. He was an unemployed twenty-something who drove by the parking lot occasionally to chat up the girls. Although nonstudents were not welcome on property, the parking lot was far away, and it was a difficult area to monitor vigilantly when the occasional dealer or underemployed lowlife would stop by. I recorded his license plate and gave it to the police. Without disclosing confidential information, they let me know that I should be concerned about him and to give them a call the next time he was on the property.

I informed Tia's mother when I heard that Tia had left school property with him. Her mother informed me that Jason was Tia's new boyfriend and she had her permission to hang out with him.

So, you can all stop riding her skinny ass.

I had a pretty crystal paperweight on my desk—a gift from a friend— and I toyed with it while on the phone. I felt its heft in my hand while I considered her words. I wondered briefly what would happen if it was thrown at the wall. Would it splinter into tiny shards or simply chip and break? I felt so frustrated by the situation.

Tia began to show up at school in the mornings only to proceed directly to the smoking area to wait for Jason. He would drive by, pick her up, and she would be gone for the rest of the day. There was nothing we could do other than inform her mother, the police, and Children's Aid—all of which we did. Her mother was clearly tired of our calls and seemed relieved Tia had finally found someone she had bonded with. She told me that Jason was good to Tia and that he had been buying her new clothes and makeup and perfume. Although all of my warning bells were ringing, her mother seemed unconcerned.

And then Tia stopped showing up at school altogether. We assumed that Jason was simply picking her up at home, and they had forgone the pretense of her attending school. We reported her absent and left messages for her mother. A week passed. Then two weeks, three, and finally six weeks. Although we had been calling home daily, her mother had not returned any of our calls.

One morning, Tia's mother showed up at school unexpectedly and walked into my office looking visibly upset. I studied her appearance. She was thin and had a grey complexion. The booze had taken its toll on her appearance. I invited her to sit and waited for her to start.

Tia's in a wack-job hospital, she said. *The cops took her.*

Where has she been?

With that shit-faced fucker, Jason.

Oh?

How in hell was I supposed to know he was a goddamn pimp?

I wanted to respond: *You SHOULD have known. I tried to warn you! I TOLD you the cops were concerned.*

But I instead spoke softly. She was a mother, and despite her tough demeanour, she was upset.

What happened? Is she alright?

No!

She began to cry, deep wracking sobs. I moved from my seat to sit beside her, bringing the tissue box close and offering it to her. Instead, she wiped at her face and nose with the sleeve of her coat, a grimy ski jacket, filthy with grease and obviously a size or two too small for her. I waited for her to continue speaking.

She was fuckin' trafficked.

What do you mean?

She went to live with him. "A couple of nights," she said. I thought, "What the hell." He seemed okay. He bought her stuff. Clothes, makeup. He took her to get her hair cut. And then he said, he needed a favour, a couple of guys were coming over, and he owed them a shitload of money, and he made her do them. And the next day it was the same. Two, three guys a night. And all the time, the ass-wipe is telling her he loves her, and she's beautiful, and so she does whatever twat-lips says. She's so goddamn stupid.

How did the police get involved?

They had a fight one night, and he fuckin' used her for a punching bag. And then he threw her the hell out. No clothes, no money, just in her goddamn underwear. The cops found her wandering the street at three in the morning, and they took her to the goddamn hospital.

Oh, my god. I'm so sorry. Now what?

The motherfuckers got him. The ass-lick of a fucker's in jail. He was feeding her shit to keep her calm. And shooting her dumbass full of something else to make her party. She'll be in the wack-job of a hospital for a couple of days.

And then what?

I don't know.

Maybe the doctors at the hospital will recommend something? Maybe there's a program somewhere that will work for Tia? Teach her some job skills.

Her mother shook her head at me.

One thing, she don't want is to come back to this lame-ass school.

We parted sadly: I offered weakly to help in any way that I could, and she indicated that school wasn't going to help her daughter. Both of us were deeply unhappy. And until that night in the grocery store, I hadn't seen or heard about Tia again.

Victoria

In the first week of school, she told me Tory was her preferred name. She thought Victoria sounded too old fashioned. She hated the name. Tory was a strong name—nothing weak or feminine or needy about someone named Tory. And that's how she began her high school career. A leggy grade nine girl with a turned-up nose and freckles who strode into my office and announced she wanted to change her name. Having met her early in the year, I continued to notice her in the halls and common areas as I made my way around the building.

Tory made the junior soccer team in the first two weeks of school. It was a good team, mostly comprised of grade ten students with space only for two grade nine students. Tory's tryout was a master class in manoeuvring quickly while maintaining speed, control, and form. No one could get the ball away from her.

I'm rather bookish and have no sports expertise, but I have spent many hours watching teenagers play all manner of games while cheering enthusiastically from the sidelines. Tory seemed to be a natural at using both feet to move the ball. Her passing wasn't bad either, but that wasn't her strong suit. It was her spatial awareness, her mastery of angles and some sort of intuitive sense of the geometry of the game where even I could see that she shone. Her tryout performance combined aggression and determination.

The team practised every morning at 7:30 a.m. I regularly dropped by the field in the mornings to watch the practice for a few minutes before heading back inside to my office. I loved the enthusiasm and energy of the girls. To remain on the team, the girls needed to maintain a 75 per cent academic average, and, as a result, they studied together, completed their homework together, and became a tight group of friends. Year after year, I had seen the positive effects of enforcing a minimum academic average for the players. They often became protective of one another. Their comradery was helpful to them as they navigated the difficult teenage years.

I met most of their parents on game day. It was the first home game of the season, and parents and grandparents came pouring onto the sidelines, carrying their coffees, and wearing our school colours. The girls were dressed in their new jerseys and shorts and were bouncing with excitement. The team we were playing had won the championship the previous year, and we knew the girls were in for a fight. They all played really well. Having family and friends on the sidelines cheering and hollering helped their performance. And Tory was a superstar. Her feet were glued to the ball. She scored three goals, helping the team to a crushing win for our side. I was proud to see the determination and evidence of the girls' tight dynamic at play.

I looked for Tory's parents after the game, but I didn't see anyone with her. It was just a small thing, but all the other girls had family members who had streamed onto the field at the final whistle to hug and congratulate them. Sports were important in a school like ours, but they weren't the only thing to keep us busy. Outside of the soccer field, I didn't really notice Tory again until later in the semester. The students were going to grade nine camp, and Tory was one of the few students who hadn't submitted her permission forms. I approached her in the hall one day and asked her about the missing forms. She flushed pink and told me that her parents hadn't signed the paperwork yet. I wondered to myself if it was a financial issue but simply encouraged her to get the forms in as quickly as possible. A week later, there were still no forms. I called home and spoke to a woman who was clearly not entirely sober.

Once I explained the reason for the call, her mother responded with *Hullo... who is this again?*

The principal of Victoria's school.

Is she in some kind of trouble?

No. No trouble. I would just like her to have the opportunity to come to camp with us.

You want to take her to camp?

Yes. With all the other grade nines.

Well, you just go ahead, darlin'. If you want to take that little mouthpiece away with you, you're welcome to her.

It's not quite that simple. I need your permission. You have to sign the forms.

I don't got no forms, darlin'. But you got my permission, fur sure.

It was a frustrating call. One of those phone conversations that made me pick up my letter opener and mock stab myself while muttering, *kill me now* with gritted teeth. I wasn't convinced that I had made any inroads, but the next morning, Tory's signed forms appeared on my desk. There was no cheque attached, but I had a contingency fund I could dip into, and I used that to cover Tory's registration fee. It felt like a satisfactory resolution. At the end of the school day, one of soccer coaches came to see me.

It's probably nothing, she said. But I thought I should mention it.

What?

Tory showed up at practice this morning with a bruise on her cheek. It looks like someone may have smacked her.

Really? It wasn't a ball?

No. I noticed before practice started.

Did you ask her about it?

She said it was nothing.

Okay, keep an eye on her and let me know if anything else happens. I'll ask someone in guidance to follow up.

That was the first sign of the physical abuse that we believed was a constant in Tory's life. Teachers reported fingerprint marks on her arms, bruises on her legs, and marks on her face. These were the surface signs we noted with concern and duly reported to Children's Aid. The underlying trauma accompanying the violence was harder for us to address. Tory was adamant that she didn't want our help. When interviewed by Children's Aid, she insisted that the marks were self-inflicted as a result of clumsiness and trips and falls. We all suspected what she would not verify, that her parents were abusive. As she was now fifteen and close to aging out, Children's Aid closed the file.

By the end of the school year, Tory was regularly couchsurfing. She mostly stayed with friends from her soccer team. The excuse given was that their parents didn't mind, and it made getting to practice really easy. Three or four nights a week, Tory was on someone's couch. Weekends were the same. She'd be invited to have a sleepover and stay for a second or third night. As a star athlete, Tory was quite popular, and her peer group gravitated towards her. She frequently appeared at school wearing one outfit in the morning only to switch clothes with a friend at lunch, modelling their new top or sweater in the afternoon.

It became fairly common knowledge in the building that Tory was afraid to go home. News of her parents' alcoholism, their subsequent unemployment, and their suspected physical abuse of her was whispered around the building. Tory spoke to a guidance counsellor in her grade ten year to ask for help in applying for social assistance. She had apparently decided she wanted to live independently from her parents and had heard somewhere that student welfare might be available.

We met with a government representative, who informed us Tory's parents would have to sign off on Tory receiving support. Her parents would have to indicate that she was no longer welcome at their home and that they were not willing to support her. Her parents would not agree to do this. They told Tory and then the government representative, that she was needed at home. Tory was certain that they believed signing off on her independence would somehow reduce their welfare cheques. She was devastated by their actions and wept with frustration. I called the board lawyer for advice.

Upon consultation, we learned that Tory could apply to become an emancipated minor, thus effectively divorcing herself from her parents. To do this, she would need a sponsor who would assume some oversight regarding her finances and living arrangements. Tory approached a couple of her teachers, asking them to become her sponsor. No one on staff was willing to take on the responsibility.

The head of girls' physical education came to my office and informed me that Tory had announced that she was quitting the team to find a part-time job so she could live on her own. She had already lined up one job at an all-night gas station and was looking for a second job. A contingent of her friends visited me in my office shortly after. They initially voiced their compassion, *How can this be happening to her*? But that was shortly followed by a less altruistic response, as they realized they would also be losing a star player from the team. In my experience, teenage girls are a complex mix of open-hearted and open-handed generosity mixed with a large dose of self-interest. This instance proved to be no different.

You have to do something! They declared, looking at me accusingly.
What would you like me to do?
You have to fix it somehow. Tory needs a safe place to live. She can't quit

the team.

Do any of you have any suggestions? Have you discussed any of this with your parents?

They shook their heads.

Maybe you should start there? Do you think that your parents might have suggestions that could help her?

The soccer collective pulled out their phones and left my office with a mission. I wasn't certain how their parents would respond, but I hoped something positive would transpire. As I suspected, several parents offered Tory places to stay temporarily. She was invited to spend a week with one girl, a weekend with another, someone else's house for another week, and so on. Each of the girls on the team offered steadfast support for Tory, including inviting her into a home, sharing their wardrobe with her, and involving her in all of the intimacies of family life. But no one would agree to become her official sponsor.

This half-solution seemed to work well enough for several months. On the rare instance when Tory had a gap between invitations, she returned home to her parents' house. Those visits did not typically end well, and the drama of her brief stay spilled over into the school. Occasionally when she returned to school, she had fresh bruising. We called Children's Aid, but Tory was now nearly sixteen, and they were unwilling to take action. I had our school liaison officer speak with her, but Tory ascribed the bruising to soccer or an incident at work. Many of us tried to impress upon her that no one had the right to hurt her and that the police could put a stop to it. Out of a sense of loyalty I could not understand, she refused to accuse her parents of the violence we believed was taking place.

In her grade eleven year, another dynamic appeared to be quietly developing. Teachers picked up on the negative chatter going around about Tory. They shared this with me out of concern for her but also from a sense of worry that escalating tensions were about to blow up. Tory and her friends were now on the senior soccer team. The group was still tightly knit, and Tory was still couchsurfing at the homes of her soccer mates. But a steady grumbling had begun to take place among her friends. Often, it had to do with Tory's ability to impress her friends' parents. She had adopted a level of artifice that was intended to curry favour. Without ever having been prompted, she cleared the dinner table and tidied the kitchen, did the laundry, walked the dog, complimented the adults, and feigned interest in their occupations.

Her friends felt that she was making them look bad in their own homes and began to resent her. Also of concern was Tory's knack of borrowing a favourite clothing item and wearing it so perfectly that it seemed to suit her better than it did its owner. Often the pieces were not returned and joined the wardrobe jumble in Tory's locker. Invitations to stay became less frequent.

Finally, just as things were heating up with peer tension and all of the ensuing drama, Tory's aunt announced she would sign off on becoming an arms-length sponsor. The emancipation process itself did not take long once sponsorship was in place. In addition to her job on the weekends, the money from social services facilitated the ability for Tory to live independently in a tiny basement apartment.

The move to her apartment coincided with what I can only describe as Tory continuing to develop a set of behaviours that came at the expense of her many friendships. She would casually mention to someone's mother that she didn't have a winter coat, for instance, and that family would buy her a coat. Tory would show up at a friend's home complaining of wet feet and no boots, and the friend's family would buy her new shoes and boots. Tory worked at a gas station on weekends, sitting alone in a glass booth collecting payments. Parents purchasing gas would regularly bring her toiletries, groceries, and small gifts. Her friends came to resent Tory and believed, rightly or wrongly, they were all being played by her. Some speculated that her parents had not abused her at all and that she had made things up to garner sympathy. The open hearts and generosity of the soccer team and their families had been liberal, but the wall of support was now showing cracks under the strain of what was perceived to be Tory's manipulation.

Traditionally, our school always held a spring sock-hop, but the student's council had successfully lobbied me for a formal so the junior grades could participate in a "dressing up" dance. There was the usual winning combination of popcorn, candy floss, brownies, a chocolate fountain, soft drinks, and flavoured potato chips. Sparkly silver stars had been hung overhead, and the fluorescent lighting in the gym had been turned off, leaving only the DJ's disco ball to illuminate the large space. Couches from the guidance area had been dragged into the hallway, and the decorating committee was thrilled with the overall effect of their efforts.

I was standing with a group of supervising teachers when Tory, wearing the shortest mini-dress I have ever seen, approached us. Standing especially tall in four-inch heels, she was wearing full makeup and had styled her hair in soft, thick waves. She sidled up to one of the male chaperones and rubbed herself against his arm. He stepped away from her, looking distinctly uncomfortable. Then she looped her arm through his and asked him for a dance. The rest of the chaperones were silent while we waited for him to respond. He casually unhooked her arm and made a joke about having two left feet. She tugged on his jacket lapels provocatively.

I'll teach you everything, she purred.

Honest to God. She purred. I'd heard of women who purred while having sex, but I had never actually heard someone make a purring sound. Blushing, he sidestepped her, and said he needed to do a tour of the parking lot. Stepping towards him more closely and deliberately brushing up against his chest, Tory ran her fingers along the front of his jacket and said, *let me come with you so you won't be afraid of the dark.*

All of us were uncomfortable with Tory's outrageously flirtatious behaviour. Staff were shifting their weight uneasily.

That won't be necessary! I interjected. *I will accompany Mr. Farrel. And you, my dear, should be in the gym dancing with your friends.*

I used my prim don't-mess-with-me voice and inserted myself between Tory and her teacher. I led him away, leaving the other staff with Tory. Both Mr. Farrel and I were quiet for several minutes. Finally, having recovered from the seductive advances, I asked whether she had done something similar before.

Uh, no. Not really. I mean, I coach the team. She high-fives me and stuff. And sometimes she wants to talk about our plays and go over the game with me. But it's all about soccer.

That's good then. You have to keep her at arm's length. She could be trouble.

I know. I'm getting that.

In grade twelve, Tory, now seventeen, quit the soccer team. She was still working two part-time jobs and still living independently. She routinely wore thick eyeliner, heavily pencilled brows, and deeply rouged cheekbones with shiny bright lip lacquer. It made her face look hardened and older. Anyone meeting her on the street or at one of her jobs would think that she was in her late twenties. Her soccer friends had closed ranks to exclude her, and she was left isolated in her final year of school. She regularly showed up late for class, exhausted from her all-night shifts and seemingly uninterested in school. Several of us tried to talk to her, but she was edgy and defensive, rebuffing all of our efforts.

I saw her walking along the highway one night. It was cold, and I slowed down to offer her a lift. She shook her head at me and kept walking along the shoulder of the road. I felt then her determination to live life on her terms. I gradually accelerated and drove by. I would like to believe that the outpouring of love, kindness, and support she had initially experienced made some sort of lasting difference in her life and that, at some point, she might come to appreciate the generosity and caring of those who had attempted to help her.

Acknowledgments

A book such as this reflects the work of so many silent friends and colleagues. First and foremost, I must pay tribute to Angie Littlefield and Bob McGary who helped to shape my administrative career in public education and taught me that administrators don't cry, they just get on with the work. I must also express my deepest appreciation to so many former colleagues—teaching staff, guidance counsellors, social workers, psychometrists, psychologists, special education resource staff, educational assistants, community liaison officers, public health nurses, Children's Aid case workers, social services workers, and faith and community partners in particular, who demonstrated such unending compassion and skill when problem solving in the service of youth.

Many thanks to Andrea O'Reilly and the team at Demeter Press who recognized the value in these stories and seek always to amplify societal issues touching upon mothering, reproduction, sexuality, and family.

Thanks also to *underthegumtree* for publishing *South End* in their Fall 2012 journal and *writers and readers magazine* for publishing a version of *The Parking Garage* in the January/February 2022 edition.

To my writing sisters Hollay Ghadery, Laura Francis, Hejsa Christensen, and AnnaLiza Kozma, I am so grateful for your encouragement and belief in this work and love the gift of each of you in my life. Thanks also to the amazing Shelley MacBeth for her work promoting and celebrating the importance of stories. With thanks also to the following friends and former colleagues for reading early drafts of this work and providing incredible support: Joe and Joyce Allin, Janet Vendrig, Judy Bear, Marlene Kadar, Gail Kirkpatrick, Carolyn Morton, Mark Joel,

Brian Jones, Martine Robinson, Michael Barrett, Jim Markovski, Heather Lutes, and Liz Roy.

And to Michael and Andrew, who lived these stories with me and provided endless support and love, as well as to my brother John, always an inspiration. You have my heart.

Deepest appreciation to
Demeter's monthly Donors

DEMETER

Daughters
Brent & Heather Beal
Carole Trainor
Khin May Kyawt
Tatjana Takseva
Debbie Byrd
Tanya Cassidy
Myrel Chernick
Marcella Gemelli
Donna Lee, In Memory of Dee Stark, RN, LNHA,
Trailblazer for Women, Women's Rights Advocate
Catherine Cheleen-Mosqueda

Sisters
Fiona Green
Paul Chu
Amber Kinser
Nicole Willey

Mother
Mildred Bennett Walker (Trainor)

Grandmother
Tina Powell